Mr Malaprop's Revenge

A Collection of Sketches, Poems,
Plays and Other Writing

by

Peter Higginbotham

© 2013 Peter Higginbotham
All Rights Reserved.

(Contents previously published under the title *Melon Cauliflowers*)
For enquires concerning public performance of any material in this collection, please contact: enquiries@peterhigginbotham.com

CONTENTS

Mr Malaprop's Revenge	1
Barefaced in the Park	4
Taking Stock	7
On the Cards	10
Melon Cauliflowers	16
DeathoGram	19
Albert at the Seaside	22
Escape	25
Acronyms	28
Fall	33
Dahlias	34
The Facts	36
Swag	37
Ilkley Moor Baht 'at (Fairtrade Version)	40
Ilkley Moor Baht 'at (International Version)	42
Week Ending	44
Steam Radio	46
Making Ends Meet	82

Mr Malaprop's Revenge

For quite a few years I was a member of the Old Gaol Theatre Company, an amateur drama group in Abingdon, Oxfordshire. It became a tradition for me to write some kind of skit on the latest production for performance at the after-show party. Sheridan's *The Rivals*, which we tackled in 2002, features the linguistically challenged widow, Mrs Malaprop. My contribution imagined the thoughts of her late (and presumably long-suffering) husband who was destined forever to remain in his wife's shadow.

> My name is Malaprop. George Malaprop. The late George Malaprop. I've been waiting for an importunity to come back and set the record straight. The facts are all recorded contemptibly here in my diarrhoea. You cannot passably reprehend how much frustration, constipation and dental anguish I have suffered since Mr Sheridan published his play 'The Rivals' over two centurions ago. Now, I ask you, whenever you mention this testicular play, who is it that people inedibly renumber, eh? Is it the radiator beauty of Lydia Languish, or the virulent and mascarpone good looks of Jock Dissolute, or the lubricating and Debenham's charms of Sir Luscious O'Trigger, or the twenty-minute high-octave sword-fight that builds up to the thrilling tampax of the final act? No, it is not. Quite on the contretemps. It is Mrs Malaprop. A dolt of a woman who couldn't even strangle two words together. Yet, inextricably, audiences go into ruptures of delight over her verbal antiques.
>
>   I can still recoil the day I first discounted the lady. It was in Westminster abbey, that great electrostatical orifice, whose vast walls are adored by carvings of the twelve opossums. As my pomade through its noble pimlicos had been somewhat cucumbered by a severe abbess on my knee, I had paused to hear

the choir who were singing without accompaniment – Acapulco – and to take refreshment at a stall where tea was being served from a great urinal. I gazed upwards to look up at the flying buttocks – those magnificent structures which mark the highest platitudes of the primeval church craftsmen's artex. Then, as I looked down, I saw the future Mrs Malaprop – a face that was to become illegibly printed on my mammary. They do say that beauty is in the eye of the bee-keeper but in that momentum I was totally capitulated by the elephant copulation of her charms. She too was mutably afflicted by my own miasma, and was soon ingratiating herself and fornicating all over me.

I learnt that she came from a very good family – her father was a wealthy typhoon and her mother some kind of civil serpent. With the insistence of a friendly gynaecologist, I looked up her family tree and discovered she was a direct decadent of King William of Pineapple. I think I can say, without fear of contraception, that I felt as happy as Michelangelo after he'd painted the sixteenth chapel. Soon afterwards, our marriage was consummated by the bishop himself at that very same altar. So many people wanted to be a wetness to our nuptials that security guards had to throw an accordion around the church.

The commensuration of our martial life together was happy and totally car-free, although I must confess that her cooking was abdominal. She did have a voluptuous book full of recipes and antidotes concerning them, but all she ever made was colostomy-flour cheese. She would tease me occasionally about my oracular perambulators and, much to my embezzlement, used to repeat them to her cousin, Mr Richard Barnsley Sheridan who then incorporated them into his latest theoretical predictions. As time passed, I discovered that my wife had humorous other unappealing hobbits. On Sunday mornings, she liked to lie in bed with a raw carrot, noisily masticating for hours on end.

Eventually, she became like an alcatraz around my neck. I had hoped she might change, but as we all know, a leper never changes his spots. I felt that I was on the horns of an enema. But she was in for a shrewd awakening.

I had a long-standing derangement to sail with a marinated friend and follow in the forceps of the great sailor Magellan on a great exhibition to circumcise the world. Our incontinent journey took us to many strange locals. In Algiers, we spent a lot of time at the cash bar. We saw the great pyramids – that range of mountains between France and Spain and, and visited Egypt where the round face of the great sphincter stands like a clock dial on the banks of the Nile. Each year, the Nile floods and irritates all the crops. We went to India where the natives wear turbines on their heads, and then crossed the specific ocean which is filled with hundreds of uninhibited islands, many of which we visited using our small and flimsy rowing boat. We attempted intercourse with many strange peoples and were frequently the receptacle of novel tongues, where cunning linguistics was required. As might naturally be infected, we picked up many monuments of our visitations. By the end of our journey, our rowlocks were totally clapped out. At last we arrived back in England and got our feet back on terracotta.

Soon after my embrocation from the ship, I was admonished to be arrested by an officer of her majesty's constabulary under a discharge of desiccating my wife. I tried to castigate the gentleman, which did little to modify his feelings. He demanded that I accommodate him to the station for further interpolation. It soon transposed that I would remain there until they had finished their incinerations. "But I am a man of great statue", I projected loudly. "And there are exterminating circumstances." I even propositioned a flea bargain, but it cut no lice. In my prison cellulite, I lay prostate with dispersion, and like Shakespeare's tragical figurine, Omelette, occasionally relieving myself in a long soliloquy. Eventually, I determined, like the great Greek ineffectual and philumenist, Socrates, to end it all – with an overdose of wedlock.

Barefaced in the Park

At the gates to the park, a man stands wearing an overlarge flower in his button-hole and carrying a copy of Time Out. *He looks at his watch and sighs. A woman, out of breath, also wearing an overlarge flower, dowdy head-scarf, and glasses appears, carrying a similar magazine. The man gives the woman a polite smile then goes back to looking at his watch and sighing. The woman surreptitiously gives the man the once-over then loses interest. The man looks at his watch and frowns.*

MAN I say, you wouldn't have the right time would you?

WOMAN Er, it's just struck half past.

MAN (*Sighs*) I was supposed to be meeting someone but it looks as if she's not coming.

WOMAN Oh, dear, I am sorry. A friend of yours?

MAN Not exactly.

WOMAN Ah.

(*Pause*)

MAN In fact – well, you see the thing is – we've never actually met before. I mean – I feel as if I've known her for years... we've corresponded you see. Exchanged, er, personal details and so on... I expect you think it all sounds a bit silly.

WOMAN Oh, no, no. Not in the least.

MAN I just know I'll recognise her instantly. She's got lots of distinctive features, you see – she's, er, sympathetic...

WOMAN I know exactly what you mean.

(*She starts to open a tube of mints*)

MAN	She's a very – sharing person...
WOMAN	Would you like a mint?
MAN	Oh thank you, that's very kind. She's – sensitive...
WOMAN	Ooh, they're jolly strong these mints aren't they.
MAN	Mmmm. She's warm-hearted....
WOMAN	(*Loosening coat*) it's been so humid today...
MAN	Romantic...
WOMAN	But it's turned into such a wonderfully clear evening. The stars are so beautiful...
MAN	Artistic...
WOMAN	Just like that painting by Reynolds...
MAN	Humorous...
WOMAN	Burt Reynolds – and he's he still making films you know.
MAN	A professional person
WOMAN	Have you got the time, dearie?
MAN	Must be twenty-five to. And to cap it all, she says she's tall, long legs and stunning looks. Well that's what her friends tell her.
WOMAN	Ah well, people put all sorts in letters. Actually, it's a really strange coincidence but I'm supposed to be meeting someone I've only corresponded with. Mine's a writer...
MAN	(*Takes out piece of paper*) You don't have a pen I could borrow, do you?
WOMAN	Well a poet, so he says...
MAN	I've thought of the headline that I need for my deadline
WOMAN	And a musician...
MAN	Just need to make a few notes.
WOMAN	Cultured...
MAN	It's for an article I doing on Beethoven's late quartets.
WOMAN	Successful...
MAN	I'm rather an authority on Beethoven, you know...
WOMAN	Modest...

MAN	Er, so people tell me…
WOMAN	Easygoing…
MAN	Not that it really bothers me either way
WOMAN	Affluent…
MAN	But I suppose it pays for the Rolls
WOMAN	Quiet…
MAN	(*Looks dreamily into the distance*)
WOMAN	And he says he's 6'3", well built, muscular and athletic.
MAN	(*Coughs and wheezes*)
WOMAN	Oh well, it doesn't look as if my friend's going to turn up either.
	(*Pause*)
BOTH	I don't suppose…
WOMAN	Sorry, after you.
MAN	No, you were first.
WOMAN	I, er, I was just wondering – as we've both been let down – whether you'd fancy coming for a drink with me
MAN	That's incredible – it's just what I was going to suggest. I mean you're not in the least like this friend of mine, but you know – I never really went for long legs.

Taking Stock

I once went on one of the excellent week-long writing courses run by the Arvon Foundation at Lumb Bank, the former home of Ted Hughes, set in magnificent Pennine isolation near the village of Heptonstall in Yorkshire. The tutors for the course ('comedy script-writing') were the chalk-and-cheese combination of David Nobbs (urbane author of 'Reginald Perrin', 'A Bit of a Do', etc.) and Alan Plater (hard-bitten writer of 'Z Cars', 'The Beiderbecke Trilogy' etc.), with David Perry ('Dad's Army', 'Are You Being Served?' etc.) putting in a guest appearance. My memories of the course are a little hazy (nothing to do with Alan's heavy smoking, I'm sure) but I recently came across what was clearly a short exercise carried out during the week which I had entitled 'Taking Stock'.

DAVID   Alan, Look... can we talk?

ALAN   Sure. (*Picks up cigarettes and lighter*) You don't mind if I...?

DAVID   I thought you were giving up.

ALAN   I am. I'm down to two of three a day.

DAVID   Is that cigarettes or packets?

ALAN   (*Lighting up*) I've told you. It helps the creativity. I mean have you ever been in a jazz club worth its name where there wasn't a haze of blue smoke hanging over the band like a blue velum parchment against which the music danced its mellifluous motifs?

DAVID   Yes. In Cambridge last week.

ALAN raises his eyebrows in an "I rest my case" kind of way.

DAVID I just wanted to say – now you've had good look at them – what do you think?

ALAN I've never seen such a load of talentless time-wasters in my life.

DAVID Isn't that a bit harsh... if you don't mind my saying so.

ALAN They wouldn't recognise a decent line if it came down carved in tablets.

DAVID What, you mean like 'Paracetamol?'

ALAN gives DAVID an "I suppose you think that's funny?" look.

DAVID Anyway, what I was going to say... I thought that redhead, what's her name – Caroline? – she sounded quite promising.

ALAN Who the bugger are you talking about David?

DAVID Caroline. The one sitting by the window. Writing the novel about the morose business executive.

ALAN Christ! I thought we were talking about the so-called actors who are this very minute desecrating my finely honed words at the West Yorkshire Playhouse.

DAVID No, I meant the...

ALAN Sorry. It's been a long day.

DAVID I know.

ALAN It wasn't like this in the old days, of course.

DAVID What, on er...

ALAN The thing about Z-cars, of course, was what you wrote was what went out. No bloody 18-year-old-I've-got-a-first-from-Cambridge – er, no disrespect David – and-the-sun-shines-out-of-my-arse script-editors in those days. I mean, I've worked with them all. Jimmy... Jerry... Jackie... Timmy... Terry...

DAVID Tacky?

ALAN Precisely.

DAVID You go back quite a way, don't you, Alan? Didn't you say you'd once worked with Noel?

ALAN   Only briefly. Then the bloody motel burnt down and it was back to Z-cars...

DAVID   (*Sighs*) Writing can certainly be a ....

ALAN   Fickle mistress?

DAVID   No....

ALAN   Capricious muse?

DAVID   No.

ALAN   Mug's game?

DAVID   That's the one. Until you reach our exalted status, of course.

ALAN   Of course.

DAVID   Er, by the way. If you don't mind me asking, what are they, er, paying you for this week?

ALAN   Oh, the usual.

DAVID   What, er, five?

ALAN   Five. You've got to be kidding. Why... is that what you get?

DAVID   Oh, no. Of course not. Oh, look, is that the time?

ALAN   No, I said I wouldn't do it for less than seven. Plus my own ashtray

DAVID   Seven, eh?

ALAN   And first pick on any good ideas they come up with. My agent's been pestering more something new for a while. I particularly like that thing the tall bloke said he's working on.

DAVID   What, the thing about the two blokes who meet up in the middle of nowhere waiting for the friend who never appears.

ALAN   That's the one. It's got everything going for it. Small cast, minimalist set, very post-modern. I reckon I could do a pretty good job on that. Could even turn it into a half-decent sitcom. I must run it past Johnny next time I see him...

DAVID   Anyway, getting back to the class – now you've had good look at them – what do you think?

ALAN   Oh them? I've never seen such a load of talentless time-wasters in my life...

On the Cards

A story told through the medium of a series of postcards.

05-AUG-94

WANTED

Flat/Bedsit/House-share in Broomfield Area for quiet graduate (non-smoker). Furnished or unfurnished.

Anything considered. References available.

Tel 298179 (ask for Pauline).

FOR SALE:-

Typewriter Smith Corona
Very Good Condition.
Types like this.

£20.

Apply Inside Shop - Mr Patel.

Hi Sis,　　　　　　　Monday 25th
Hope you like the card (sorry, couldn't find a
Welcome-To-Your-New Home one!) – Oxford
really is full of bikes. People on course v. nice
and my tutor's v. dishy!! Mum says you finally
got yourself a typewriter – THE GREAT NOVEL??
New start is just what you need so just you get
out there and show 'em!!!
Write soon, love Val xxx
P.S. Miaows to Sammy.

```
                                           30-SEP-94

   *** IT'S AS EASY AS... UN, DEUX, TROIS!***

   One-to-one French tuition by experienced
                    graduate.

                Only £5 per hour.

     Phone Pauline on 484139 anytime.

                  ---o-O-o---
```

The Shaftsbury Clinic　　　Date as Postmark

Dear Ms Woods,
An appointment has been arranged for you at the clinic on <u>27th October</u> at <u>3.30pm</u>.

Please do not eat for <u>6</u> hours beforehand.
If you are unable to keep this appointment, please telephone 435687 to rearrange it.

07-OCT-94

**** FRENCH TRAVEL? BUSINESS? EXAMS? ****

<u>French language lessons</u>,
exam coaching,
conversation,
translation work etc.

Personal service offered by graduate.
<u>Only £4 per hour.</u>

Tel. P Hopkins 484139.

25-OCT-94

FOR SALE.

Wedding Dress, ivory satin. Size 16.
Never worn. £45 ono.

Matching shoes, size 7. £10.

Tel. 484139.

10-NOV-94

HELP!!

LOST - Broomfield Rd area.

'Sammy' - small ginger & white cat
(female, grey collar, piece missing
from left ear).

Tel. 484139.

```
                                              15-NOV-94

            * PUT YOUR FEET UP!*

Typing? Gardening?
Baby-sitting? Dog-Walking?
Cleaning? etc. etc.

Reliable, versatile graduate seeks work, odd
jobs. Anything Considered.

Tel. Pauline on 484139.
```

Nov 28th 1994

Dear *Mr Wood*

This is to acknowledge receipt of your poems for ***Furry Friends*** magazine. We shall keep them on file in case we are ever able to use them in a future issue.

Yours sincerely,
Julia Jellicoe
Editor-in-chief.

```
                                              03-DEC-94
           +-+-+-+-+ FOR SALE +-+-+-+-+

       Typewriter (Smith Corona) £25 o.n.o.
                 Types like this.

    Assorted French text books, dictionaries,
 novels, magazines etc. - very good condition.

           Any reasonable offers accepted.

                Tel 484139 anytime.
```

Hi Sis,   10th December
Wish you were here! The Alps are totally gorgeous (and so is Mike!!) Really sorry about cancelling my trip up to see you at such short notice but this was an offer I just couldn't refuse. Hope things are still going well with you. Looking forward to reading some of the great novel!! See you at Mum and Dad's on the 25th.
Lots of love Val xxx.

12-DEC-94

FRENCH LESSONS? OOH LA LA!!

<u>Experienced</u> lady offers <u>personal</u> French tuition. All requirements catered for.

If your French needs some polishing, let's make a rendezvous today!

Mademoiselle Pauline. Tel 484139.

17-DEC-94

<u>REWARD</u>

Offered to finder of small ginger and white cat with grey collar and piece missing from left ear.

Answers to the name of Sammy.
Lost in Broomfield Rd area, approx. 5 weeks ago.

Tel. 484139.

> 24th Dec
>
> Dear Mr Patel,
>
> This is just to say I am going away.
> If my cat Sammy turns up, could you try and see he is looked after. Thanks very much for all the help with the postcards in your window.
>
> Pauline Woods.

> Christmas Eve
>
> Dear Mum and Dad and Val,
> I'm so sorry for the awful pain and distress I know this will cause you but I just can't go on any longer. I know you always had such high hopes for me but I seem to have let you down at every step and I've just had enough.
> Please forgive me.
> God bless you all.
> Pauline

Melon Cauliflowers

BASIL and LILY have been having a tiff in the garden....

BASIL   Lily, what's the matter? All I said was I thought you were getting a bit obsessed with the garden. I suppose this is going to be one of your haughty, cultural phases. All you seem to think about these days is grass, grass, grass. You know what they call you – lovelawn.

LILY   Basil – I know you're jealous of my grass, but I can do without you hovering around, making all these cutting remarks. I just have to mention that the grass is too long and it's mown, mown, mown. It's much better than that old stuff we turfed out.

BASIL   (*To himself*) Silly old sod.

LILY   (*To herself*) And you're pasture best

BASIL   What was that, oh apple of my eye?

LILY   Nothing, my sugarplum. I was just thinking that, of the pear of us, you are the elder. Now did you prune that shrub like I told you to? We want to make sure it sprouts new shoots.

BASIL   Prunes and sprouts, prunes and sprouts. That's all I ever get from you.

LILY   What do you mean?

BASIL   It's a dahlia currents.

LILY   Oh, and by the way, you old rake...

BASIL   (*Sarcastically*) Hoe, Hoe

LILY   Never mind the hose – pipe down will you.

BASIL   Well what's nettling you now? Come on, don't beat about the bush.

LILY   You've still not fetched the hedge-clippers back from the repairer's. Shear laziness!

BASIL   The man next door's got some – wheel barrow his.

LILY	Well, we mustn't rest on our laurels. I'll rush and see him straight away.
BASIL	Oh, no you don't – you know he's sweet on you.
LILY	Sweet? William! You know, I can barley believe you'd say such a thing. You get madder every day. All because I said I was taken by the hollyhocks behind his compost bin...
BASIL	He's always trying it on – I've heard about the forays at the bottom of his garden. Last time, he weedled you into his greenhouse to look at his tomato trusses. And you couldn't stop talking about the big squash he gave you.
LILY	Well he did offer to plant a few seeds in my front bed with his dibber. And do a bit of pricking out on the side. There's nothing Willie likes more than a good prick-out. He says his peonies could stand some attention. And he's got some French lettuce he wants to show me if he gets the opportunity.
BASIL	Oh, I bet he has. Well, I think he deserves a jolly good patio on the back. Universal Pansy!
LILY	He's an inspiration to all budding gardeners. It all stems from his very fertile imagination.
BASIL	Creeping Bindweed!
LILY	Do calm down Basil. You know what the doctor said. You don't want another artichoke.
BASIL	Don't you worry. I'm still perfectly compost mentis.
LILY	Anyway, you're no saint Basil... let's not forget that Poppy of yours
BASIL	I was wondering when you'd dig that up again.
LILY	You always said you'd bee-troot to me.
BASIL	It was all a long time ago.
LILY	It was so awful, to see her-becide you, in the meadow amongst the phlox with your buttock-up. It made that poor cow slip.

BASIL   Actually, we were just on the verge. She told me to li-lac and enjoy it. I don't know what came over me. It was just a sudden wisteria.

LILY   I should have nipped it in the buddleia. You were lucky you didn't end up in the dock. If it were up to me, I'd freesia bulbs.

BASIL   So – I manure bad books, am I? Oh, I do pine fir your forgiveness, Lily.

LILY   I know I sometimes bark up the wrong tree and make you bough to my views. Perhaps I should branch out and take a leaf out of Hazel's book.

BASIL   Which Hazel? Oh, the kernel's daughter.

LILY   (*About to sneeze*) uh... uh... cashew!

BASIL   Oh Lily, you know I'm nuts about you. Look – thistle cheer you up – the clematis is just coming out.

LILY   I love the clematis – it's such a melon cauliflower.

BASIL   (*Warmly*) Oh, and you're such a Belladonna, Lily. Cumquat may, I am glad I picked you.

LILY   (*They hold hands*) Time for tea?

BASIL   (*Bends down and picks up a sprig*) Thyme for tea!

DeathoGram

That was the part of the job I hated most. The one thing they didn't prepare you for. And no matter how many times you did it, it never seemed to get any easier.

I turned right at the lights into Lombard Street. Here we go. Number twenty-two. Halifax House. One of those modern office buildings with exposed chunks of girder painted bright red and blue. Pull into the visitors' parking area and turn off the engine. At least it hadn't been too difficult finding the place. I opened my pouch and took out a lip-stick. Dawn Mist. Just a quick touch-up and a tidy of the hair under the cap. Nothing too ostentatious though – you always have to look the part in this job or people don't take you seriously, especially if you're a woman.

I looked at my notebook again to check the details. Mr John Lawrence, Holcroft Associates. Drawing Office, Second Floor, 25th March, 10am. I checked my watch. It was just gone five to.

I tried to decide how I would break the news to him. Up front and on the chin, or going all round the houses so he'd more or less work it out for himself. That's what people seemed to prefer on the whole. And it sort of let me off the hook, not actually having to say the words.

I approached the reception window and pressed the button. The frosted glass panel slid open to reveal a middle-aged woman in a cream blouse with a high collar. 'You're here for Mr Lawrence,' she announced, 'I'll show you up, officer.' I was obviously expected.

The second floor was a large open-plan office. Over towards the window, sitting at a large drawing-board, sat John Lawrence. He was younger than I'd anticipated, with fair hair and wearing heavy brown-framed glasses. He seemed quite taken aback to see me, almost jumped off his chair. 'Look, if it's about the TV licence, I keep telling you people that – incredible as it may seem – we actually don't have a set. You're welcome to come and look, you know.'

Oh well, nothing for it. I launched into my routine. 'Mr Lawrence, Mr John Lawrence? Number 15, The Poplars?'

'Yes?'

I could see that sizeable audience had already gathered around us.

'I'm afraid I've some rather bad news for you.'

'Oh, no. Is it my father?'

'No sir, it's your wife. I think you'd better sit down.' There was the sound of a stifled snigger behind me. I took a deep breath. 'When did you see her last?'

'This morning. She was driving the kids to... Oh God, what's happened?'

His face had turned white and he looked terrified. Around me, the chorus of whispers and titters was growing. I wanted to scream at them to shut up. They were supposed to be adults. Did they really think this was funny? Did they actually imagine I was enjoying this?

'Well, you see sir, the thing is...' It was at the moment I bottled out. 'The thing is, sir, the thing is... er, she's... eloped to South America with the window-cleaner and she asked us to come and tell you your dinner's in the microwave. In the meantime...'

Then, to a cacophony of raucous cheers and applause, I pulled open the velcroed fastenings on my jacket and skirt, dropped them to the floor and jumped on to the lap of the now totally bewildered draughtsman. Behind the frozen grin on my face I felt like throwing up. In fact, I don't know how I didn't.

And that was the last DeathoGram I ever did, or rather didn't do. The guy who had paid for it gave me a really hard time. He complained to the company saying if he'd wanted a clapped-out old stripogram, he'd have gone elsewhere and paid half the price. The bastard. I really needed that job.

Then, last week, I discovered that his grandmother lives on our estate, on Kelsall Drive. I'm just on my way now to pay her a call. Better just touch up my make-up. Nothing too ostentatious though – you have to look the part or people don't take you seriously.

Albert at the Seaside

I've always been very fond of the humorous monologue, and also the parody – the two forms perhaps most notably combined by the 1920s' music-hall star, Billy Bennett in such classics as 'The Green Tie on the Little Yellow Dog' (his take on 'The Green Eye of the Yellow God'). One of my own essays into the genre was inspired by Stanley Holloway's immortal rendering of the 'Albert and the Lion', adapted to setting with rather more present-day relevance – the nuclear waste reprocessing plant at Sellafield in Cumbria.

> There's a famous seaside place called Sellafield,
> That's noted for nuclear waste.
> And Mr and Mrs Ramsbottom
> And their son went to visit the place.
>
> A grand little lad were young Albert,
> In his tracksuit and trainers, right nice.
> And a Sony Stereo Walkman
> From Woolworths, last Christmas, half price.
>
> They didn't think much to the ocean,
> The sea were all frothy and pink.
> There were no fish, no birds and no people –
> Why, it almost made you think.
>
> So, seeking for some entertainment,
> They visited nuclear plant
> Where they'd particles, X-rays and ions,
> And other delights to enchant.
>
> Now Albert had heard about ions
> And how they're kept safe as can be,
> So he goes through a door marked 'No Admission'
> (He just thought it meant it were free).

Inside were all pipes and ladders,
And dials and buttons to push.
So Albert, being an inquisitive lad,
Tries them all out in a rush.

An alarm bell then begins ringing
And folks all around start to run,
But Albert, still wearing his Walkman,
Were quite unaware of the fun.

At the snack bar, Mr Ramsbottom
Were asking the woman 'What's these?'
'Oh they're called Sellafield Sandwiches –
They're made with re-processed cheese'.

On the Tannoy comes an announcement
That although nothing was wrong,
All visitors had to leave pronto,
So please could they hurry along.

'Where's Albert?' cried Mother in panic,
'I thought he's too quiet to be true.
I hope he's not got into mischief,
And him in his new trainers too.'

A chap in a white coat assured them
It was only a practice drill.
But another one kept on muttering
About something called 'Chernobyl'.

The daylight was fading quite quickly,
But Ramsbottoms were demanding the truth.
Then out of the darkness before them
Emerged a luminous youth.

It had finally dawned on young Albert
That something wasn't quite right
When his stereo headphones had melted
And his tracksuit gave off a green light.

The men from the plant were quite sorry
The Ramsbottoms had had such upset.
They refunded their admission money
And asked to forgive and forget.

The newspapers later reported
An amount (microscopically small)
Of nuclear stuff was emitted,
But no staff were affected at all.

It was also untrue, said a spokesman,
That they now disposed of their waste
By selling gift packs to the tourists
Who came to visit the place.

Now when Albert recalls his adventure
That fateful day at the seaside,
Beneath his stereo headphones
He really glows with pride.

Escape

I twist the old man's head this way and that, but it won't go into the hole. His glassy grey eyes are leering up at me, mocking my efforts. Nearby, a bell starts to ring and the distant babble of voices is getting nearer. It's no good. I can't go on any longer. I sigh and push the jigsaw away from me towards the foot of the bed. I can never concentrate on anything at visiting time.

I usually spend the hour watching the clock above the double doors, counting down the minutes till four o'clock when the solicitous multitudes, relieved of their floral and fructal offerings, are finally chivvied out of the ward. Not that I ever get any visitors, thank God. All that platitudinous prattle about how you'll soon be back on your feet, what's the food like, and has that Nurse MacIntyre given you a blanket-bath yet.

'Mr Graham?' To the left of my bed stands a man in his mid-twenties, fresh-faced, and sprucely turned out in a well-cut blue suit, white shirt and tie. He is carrying a brief-case. He looks like a salesman.

'Yes?' I reply involuntarily.

'Michael Richie.' He extends a hand. 'Hospital League of Friends gave me your name. They say you don't get too many visitors.' He speaks with a slight American accent.

I raise an index finger in minimal acknowledgement. Any visitor is one too many as far as I'm concerned. 'I get quite enough,' I reply. Without being invited, he has already sat himself down in my bedside chair. I raise half an eyebrow. 'I do hope you're not selling anything, Mr Richie.'

'Mike. Please, call me Mike. No, I'm no salesman, Derek – it's OK if I call you Derek?' Without waiting for a response, he carries on.

'Well, Derek, you know it's strange you should mention it – but that's exactly what I was in my former life, a salesman. A pretty successful one at that, if I may say so. Big car, big apartment, you name it. And I was happy – at least I thought I was. But deep down inside, if I was honest, there was something missing. You know what I mean?'

I smile politely and feign a large yawn. 'I'm sorry Mr Richie, I'm feeling very tired. I wonder if you'd mind...' But he doesn't take the hint.

'Now, Derek, I can tell you're a pretty astute guy and I expect you're probably saying to yourself, "Mike, that's all well and good, but how does it relate to me?" Well, you see Derek, in the Holy Bible we are told that Jehovah God spoke to his prophets and He said, "My people, I have made you in mine own image."'

Oh my God, he's a religious nutcase. I'm trapped in bed with a heart condition and sitting in a chair two feet away from me is a raving religious maniac.

'In His own image, Derek. In His own image! Now can you honestly tell me that the God of all creation suffers from depression and cancer and strokes and heart attacks? No, of course you don't. That would be crazy. So what does it mean?'

How dare he waltz in here spouting all this twaddle. My heart is pounding. I can feel the tension tightening around my chest. 'I'm sorry, Mr Richie, I need to use a bedpan. Would you mind getting the nurse?'

'The simple self-evident truth is that all our so-called illness and disease is purely an illusion of the mortal mind. As soon as we understand that basic fact, all suffering will cease. Even death shall hold no dominion.'

He's not listening to a word I'm saying. I'm getting breathless. My fists are clenched. My pyjamas are soaked with sweat.

'Please, Mr Richie. Mike. Please, I need to rest.'

'We won't need drugs, blood transfusions, operations, or hospitals even. The power of God's love is there, ours for the taking, waiting to illuminate our darkness and to save our souls from eternal torment...'

Something finally snaps inside me. My eyes close. My whole body arches and writhes, and the jigsaw tray is thrown from the bed scattering its contents over my visitor. It lands with a crash on the hard floor. I clasp my pillow across my chest and a stream of strangulated screams erupts from my mouth. There are footsteps, voices, and the sound of curtains being drawn around my bed. After a few moments, I slowly peek out from behind the pillow to find a familiar face looking down at me.

'Has he gone?' I ask sheepishly.

Nurse MacIntyre sighs and shakes her head. 'Yes, Mr Graham, he's gone.'

Acronyms

Some years ago, *The Observer* newspaper ran a feature where the names of countries, cars, composers etc. were rendered as appropriate acronyms. Here are a few of my own submissions. My acronym for AUSTRALIA was subsequently 'borrowed' by Kathy Lette and used in her novel *Foetal Attraction*.

Birds

ALBATROSS – A Large Bird Attracting Troubled Rimer On Sailing Ship
CUCKOO – Casts Unwanted Caterwauling Kids On Others
MAGPIE – Many A Glittering Piece Is Extracted
ROBIN – Red Overcoat Brings It Notice
STORK – Specialised Transportation Of Recent Kids
TURKEY – Thousands Usually Require Killing Each Yuletide
VULTURE – Very Useful Land Tidier: Unsavoury Remains Eaten

Cars

BMW – Big Macho Wheels
ESCORT – Entices Sexy Companions On Rallying Trips
FIAT – Feel It's All Tinfoil
LADA – Laughed At Driving Around
LOTUS – Loads Of Throbbing Unhibited Sex
METRO – Midgets Enjoy The Roomy Opulence
MORGAN – Marvellous Old Roadster Generating Awful Noise
RELIANT – Rare Experience Like Inside A Nippy Tin-can
ROVER – Runs On Very Expensive Refills
SAAB – Smorgasbord Available At Back
SKODA – Some Kind Of Disaster Area
VOLVO – Vehicle Of Loathsome Vulgar Ostentation

Composers
BACH – Brilliantly Advertising Cigars (Hamlet)
BRAHMS – Bragged Relentlessly About His Musical Staff
CHOPIN – Cunning Handiwork On Piano In Nocturnes
ELGAR – Edward Left Gerontius Asleep Rhapsodically
GERSHWIN – George's Energetic Rhythms Sure Helped Words Ira Noted
HANDEL – Heralded A New Drink Entitled Largo
ROSSINI – Ravishing Operas Superbly Sung In Neapolitan Italy
SCHUBERT – Such Clever Harmonies Underlie Beautifully Evocative Romantic Tunes
WAGNER – Was A Greater Nibelung Ever Realised?

Countries
AUSTRALIA – An Uncouth Society Treats Royalty Almost Like Its Aborigines
FRANCE – François Rails Against Non-Committed English
CHINA – Communist Hierarchy Is Now Ascendant
ENGLAND – Empire Now Gone Leaving Absolute National Decay
GERMANY – Great Empire's Reunification May Awaken Nazi Yearnings
HONG KONG – Home Of Numerous Great Kings Of Novelty Goods
SWEDEN – Stockholm Women Enjoy Dating Energetic Norwegians

Drinks
TEA – The English Addiction
COFFEE – Cups Of Foaming Froth – Espresso Expensivissimo
GIN – Granny's Inebriated Nightly
LAGER – Low Appeal Gassy Emetic Recipe
MEAD – Monks Enjoyed A Drop
PERRIER – Pretentious Exhibitionists Refill Regularly In Elegant Restaurants
PUNCH – Partygiver's Usual Nauseously Concocted Horror
VODKA – Virtually Only Drink Kremlin Approves

Musical Instruments

CELLO – Catgut Emissions Launch Lloyd-Webber Ovation
CYMBAL – Can't You Make Bash Any Louder?
DRUM – Din Really Upset Mother
GUITAR – Gets Untalented Individuals Tremendous Audience Reaction
HARP – Has Always Required Pluck
HORNPIPE – Heard On Royal Navy Parades, It Penetrates Everywhere
OBOE – Off Beat Orchestral Effects
ORGAN – Ours Really Generates Appalling Noises
TRIANGLE – Tapped Rhythmically, Its Accented Notes Generate Little Expression
TROMBONE – The Raucous Outpourings May Bring On Nervous Exhaustion
TUBA – Tubing's Unwieldy Balancing Act

Occupations

CHEF – Cook Hoping Egon's Favour
CHEMIST – Condoms Have Expanded Magnificently (In Sales Terms)
DENTIST – Drills Enthusiastically – Need Tranquiliser If Seeing Tariff
DUSTMAN – Drops Unsecured Stuff To Mess Attractive Neighbourhood
ESTATE AGENT – Expertly Sells Tumbledown Attic (Translation: Exquisite Apartment) Grossly Exploiting New Tenants
FARMER – Failed Agricultural Reforms Mean Extra Revenue
MINER – Man In Nearly Extinct Role
PILOT – Proficient In Landing On Tarmac
PLUMBER – Pipes Left Unlagged May Burst – Expensive Repair!
POLITICIAN – Person Of Low Integrity Takes In Constituents – It's A Nightmare
PROSTITUTE – Post Requiring Outgoing Sort That's Inclined To Undertake The Exposure
TEACHER – Talented Educator All Children Hold Extremely Respectfully

Publications

FT – Flesh Toned
GUARDIAN – Gives Us A Rare Dislpay In Accruate Nesw
MIRROR – Maxwell's Incredible Rackets Ripped Off Readers
OBSERVER – Oh Boy, Such Excellent Reading Value – Easily Recommended
PUNCH – Provides Unique Nerve-Calming Humour
STAR – Sex Tales About Royalty
SUN – Sleazy Unappetising Nonsense
TIMES – Thunderer – In Murdoch's Era Spiritless
VIZ – Vulgarity Is Zany

Small Beasts

ANT – Attacks Nether Territory
BEE – Buzzes Energetically Everywhere
FLEA – Felines Launch Epidermal Assault
GREENFLY – Gardeners Rapidly Eradicate Excessive Numbers Fearing Low Yields
MOTH – Munches On Tasty Hems
SNAIL – Strong-stomached Nibble At Its Limbs
SPIDER – Screams Provoked If Dares Enter Room

Sports and Games

ANGLING – A Neat Gadget Lures In Naive Grayling
BOWLS – Balls Older Women Like Seizing
BRIDGE – Bidding Rules Impose Difficulty – Get Experience
CRICKET – Concealed Rubbing Incites Controversy Kindling English Tempers
DARTS – Do Alcoholics Really Throw Straight?
GOLF – Grassed-Over Lumpy Fields
POLO – Pots Of Lolly Obligatory
SKIING – Snowmen Kip In Igloos Near Glacier
WHIST – Wonderful Hand If Spades Trumps

Towns and Cities

BATH – Brilliant Austen Tarried Here

BLACKPOOL – Beautiful Landladies Are Charming, Kindly People Offering Overwhelming Luxury

BIRMINGHAM – British Industry Really Made Its Name Great Here At Middle

BOGNOR – 'Bugger,' Old George (Nearly Over) Retorted.

COVENTRY – City Organises Very Explicit Nude Tableau, Repeated Yearly

EPSOM – Effervescent Powdered Salts Overcome Meagreness

HULL – Housed Unconforming Larkin's Library

LONDON – Lots Of Nasty Dirt, Odour, Noise

MANCHESTER – Many A Northern Cricketer Has Experienced South Trafford's Endless Rain

SLOUGH – Strange Laureate's Offer – Unleash Grenades Here!

STOKE – Suffers Tons Of Kiln Emissions

YORK – Ye Olde Rowntree Kingdome

Fall

I worked in Oxford for many years. Here are some impressions of the onset of autumn there in 1994.

October days are a special time. Damp, smoky mornings reveal the black-shrivelled limbs of soft fleshed plants succumbed to the first frosts. Dew-spangled cobwebs catch watery shafts of sunlight as their owners huddle out of site in the recesses of the porch. Fresh fallen conkers with their boot-gleaming sheen await their fate at the hands of approaching schoolboys.

By lunchtime, the sun is glazing down on the bed of red, orange, yellow and pink-petalled begonias in front of the war memorial. The tourists have moved on and the undergraduates have taken their place. After the choking coach-fumes of summer, St Giles is now awash with bicycles. A long-legged, black-tighted, short-skirted woman rides past, unintentionally causing a three-car pile-up at the give-way sign. A unicyclist, his face tense with concentration (or perhaps, a studied nonchalance) pedals past. His machine seems to have no brakes and I fantasise what would happen if I leapt out in front of him. When winter comes, will he juggle snowballs with one hand and hold aloft a multi-coloured umbrella with the other?

Then by four o'clock, the sun is slinking away and a chilling wind swirls the first autumn leaves. As I stare out of the window, my thoughts turn to tea and toast. And you.

Dahlias

One of my father's great pleasures was gardening. The back garden of our council house, a former orchard, had quite heavy soil and it took him a while to find anything that would grow successfully. He tried potatoes but gave up that idea after my mother – who lacked any of the patience that he had in abundance – kept digging them up to see if they were ready yet. He then discovered a plant that loved our soil – dahlias.

> The back garden of our house in Blenheim Road
> Used to be a big orchard, so my Dad always said.
> We just had these two tall pear trees and a rickety old apple.
> When the pears were ready, he threw a rope over a branch,
> Tied a small bucket to one end and my red pedal car to the other.
> When I drove forward, the bucket lifted to catch some fruit.
>
> There was a long path up the middle of the garden.
> Lawn on the left and the soil on the right where the dahlias went
> In long lines, each with a thick bamboo cane for it to grow up.
> Every row was planted with a different variety —
> Gerrie Hoek, Cheerio, My Love, Gloria Van Heemsted,
> And lots of others whose names now escape me.
>
> Dahlias flowers come in all sorts of colours and shapes –
> Red and yellow, pink and purple, orange and white.
> Some even have different coloured stripes.
> There are cactus ones, and decoratives and pompons,
> And earwigs like to hide in the flowers and come out at night.
> My brother said they crawl up your nose or into your ear.
>
> Dahlias have these big fat roots called tubers.
> In the autumn you dig them up and chop off the stems,
> And wash the tubers with the hose pipe and let them dry out.
> Then you put them away in the loft in cardboard boxes
> With a little metal label tied on each tuber
> So you'll be able to remember which one's which.

The next year, when you take them out of their boxes,
They have pale shoots sprouting from the tubers.
You cut them up with a hacksaw and plant them again
And you end up with lots more than you had last year.
Sometimes, a few of the tubers have gone mouldy
And you have to throw them away.

Our dahlias were so good that people used to come and buy them,
They cost two and six for a huge great big bunch.
One day a lady came for a bunch of just red and white ones —
They were for the church or something she said.
My Dad thought it was dead funny and asked her why –
Didn't God like all the other colours, he wanted to know.

In the winter, I used to dig a hole in the soil —
A really deep hole, as tall as me, down to the sand.
If you keep going you'll reach Australia, my Dad used to say.
One day, at dinner time when I was in the house,
My brother got some coal and buried it in the hole
For me to find when I started digging again.

I went running into the house, all excited
Because I thought I'd discovered a coal mine.
It's one of those stories my Dad always liked to tell,
Like me feeding the loaf to the horse over the back fence,
Or that time they had to call out the plumber
Because I'd blocked the toilet with a baked bean tin.

My Dad said that his Dad used to grow dahlias,
And his Granddad – on an allotment in Birmingham,
So I suppose it's a kind of family tradition.
When I grew up and had my own garden
I tried growing dahlias myself for a bit but the nice ones
Always seemed to go mouldy, so I've sort of given up.

The Facts

Despite the fact that you demand my honest opinion about your new shoes then get upset if I give it to you.
Despite the fact that you say size isn't important then ask me if I've realised my bald patch is getting bigger.
Despite the fact that you always put down tampons on the shopping list when it's my turn to go to Tesco's.
Despite the fact that while we're making love you ask me if it was socks or gloves we gave Uncle Jack last Christmas.
Despite the fact that you gave Oxfam my favourite purple cord jeans that I haven't worn for three years.
Despite the fact that when you get into bed your feet are always freezing whatever the weather.
Despite the fact that you aren't impressed when I inform you that we're actually standing on the second longest railway platform in Wales.
Despite the fact that I'm even less impressed when you inform me that red peppers contain masses more vitamins than apples or oranges.
Despite the fact that no matter how meticulously I make the bed it never comes up to your rigorous standards.
Despite the fact that you didn't exactly go overboard on the oven glove I bought you for your last birthday.
Despite the fact you always want to know why there aren't any father-in-law jokes (then ask me to explain that bit about when the Irish priest got out of the railway carriage and the Jewish rabbi got in).
Despite all that (and that's just the half of it).
Despite all that (and that's the weird part of it).
Despite all reason, despite everything, despite myself... I love you.

Swag

A man carrying a sack climbs through the window into bedroom where girl is sleeping. A large Christmas stocking is hanging up near her bed. The man puts his sack down and starts rummaging through a drawer.

GIRL	(*Sits up with a start and pulls duvet up to her chin*) Who'th there!
MAN	Oh my gawd.
GIRL	Who ith it? Ith that you Daddy? I'm fwightened.
MAN	Er, don't be afraid, little girl. I ain't gonna hurt ya. Just put a sock in it and everything'll be alright.
GIRL	I don't have any thmelly thockth. Just my big Cwithmath thtocking hanging up there waiting for... Thanta, it'th you!
MAN	Eh? What? Oh Yurr, that's right. Huh, I'm Favver Chrismas, ho-ho-ho.
GIRL	You don't look like Father Cwithmath. He wearth a big red coat and a red hat not a funny black mathk and thtwipey thirt.
MAN	Ah well ya see, er, this is me working clobber. That red getup is me, er, ceremonial outfit, see. Oh well, nice meetin' ya. I'd better me on me way. Er, ho-ho-ho.
GIRL	Pooh. Your bweath thmellth all funny. Juth like when my Daddy comth home from a buthineth conthultanthy theminar – at the Dog and Fewet.
MAN	Oh, the Ferret, eh – I drops in there meself sometimes for a swift – business consultancy seminar. Oh, well give him my regards. Ho-ho-ho.
GIRL	What'th in that big thack? Ith it full of pwethenth?
MAN	Sack? What sack? Oh – that sack! Yurr, I'm, er, just on me rounds deliverin' presents to all the nice kiddies what keeps stumm and don't wake up the whole flamin' house. Gorrit?

GIRL	Why doeth your thack thay TH-W-A-G on it?
MAN	Wot? Oh, so it does. Well, that's a very good question that is. I'm glad you asked me that. Er, THWAG – I mean, SWAG – it's sort of the motto of my trade, ya see. It's er, I know – it's – Seasonal Wishes An' Greetin's.
GIRL	And have you got thomething thuitably theathonal thtuffed in your thack for me, Thanta?
MAN	Oh, no – I don't think I've got anything you'd like. Anyhow, I'd better go – the getaway car – er, I mean the reindeer will be wonderin' where I am.
GIRL	I want a pwethent! If you don't gimme a pwethent I'll thwceam and thwceam and thcweam till I'm thick. And I bet you I can. Thow me what'th in your thack.
MAN	Blimey! Oh all right.
GIRL	Let me thee. Oooh, a diamond necklath. Thilver kniveth and forkth. A bottle of whithky. Video camewa. Cuddly toy. What a lot you've got – you have got a lot. I'll have all of thothe.
MAN	You can't have 'em all – ya little ba- ba- ba-
GIRL	Black sheep? Oh yeth I can. I alwayth get whatever I want. I'm nearly gwown-up – my daddy thayth I'm a little madam.
MAN	But I can't go home empty 'anded. The missus'll kill – I mean, er – there's all the other dear little boys and girls to deliver presents to.
GIRL	Oh, all wight. Here you are.
MAN	Wot – the cuddly toy. Oh thank you very much.
GIRL	Don't mention it. This video camewa'th lovely – I want to try it out. You must thing a thong for me before you go.
MAN	Leave it out. What do fink this is – bleedin' auditions for Briatin's Got Talent?
GIRL	I'll thcweam!
MAN	All right!

GIRL	My favourite'th Kylie Minogue. You must thing me one of her thongth.
MAN	I don't fink I know her...
GIRL	(*Takes deep breath*)
MAN	All right! (*Very quietly*) I should be so lucky...
GIRL	Louder.
MAN	(*Slightly louder*) I should be so lucky...
GIRL	Louder!
MAN	Lucky, lucky, lucky.
GIRL	And the actions!
MAN	(*Haphazardly waving arms.*) Lucky, lucky, lucky
GIRL	All right that'th enough. You can go now. And thank you for all the lovely pwethenth, Thanta.
MAN	Oh don't mention it. (*He exits*)
GIRL	(*Picks up phone then dials. Speaks in adult voice*) Hello – police? I've just been burgled. No just a teddy bear. But I managed to get him on video and I've got his finger prints on some knives and forks. You'll come straight away. Good. (*Puts phone down – back to girl's voice.*) Hee-hee-hee-hee. I thould be tho lucky, lucky, lucky, lucky...

Ilkley Moor Baht 'at (Fairtrade Version)

In January 2013, the designation of Yorkshire as the UK's first Fairtrade region was marked by a number of celebrations across the county including one at Ilkley. As the basis of a musical contribution to the proceedings, I was asked to pen some new lyrics to the Yorkshire anthem 'On Ilkley Moor Baht 'at' which were performed for the occasion by the local community choir Ilkley Moornotes.

> From Ilkley Moor to Pickering,
> From Scarborough to Sheffield,
> Yorkshire's supporting trade that's fair –
> Showing producers that we care.
> We'll pay an honest price
> For cotton, tea and rice –
> Yes, Yorkshire's for Fairtrade.
>
> From Penistone to Doncaster,
> From Rotherham to Richmond,
> Yorkshire's supporting trade that's fair –
> Showing producers that we care.
> Sustainable bananas,
> And sugar and sultanas –
> Yes, Yorkshire's for Fairtrade.
>
> From Leeds to Thornton and Burley,
> From Beverley to Bradford,
> Yorkshire's supporting trade that's fair –
> Showing producers that we care.
> Helping to ease the toil
> In making juice and oil –
> Yes, Yorkshire's for Fairtrade.

From Otley, Baildon and Shipley,
To Harrogate and Ripon,
Yorkshire's supporting trade that's fair –
Showing producers that we care.
Fairtrade means opportunities
To improve their communities –
Yes, Yorkshire's for Fairtrade.

From Cherry Burton to Bingley,
From York to Hull and Haworth,
Yorkshire's supporting trade that's fair –
Showing producers that we care.
And so we say with pride,
The Fairtrade Mark's our guide –
Yes, Yorkshire's for Fairtrade.

[*All the places mentioned are Fairtrade towns or villages in Yorkshire.*]

Ilkley Moor Baht 'at (International Version)

'Ilkley Moor Baht 'at' has recently been the subject of a campaign to introduce the song to younger Yorkshire folk who, apparently, no longer learn it at their mother's knee. For those living outside 'God's Own County', the dialect lyrics of the song's ten or so verses – a tale of the consequences of a hatless foray onto the moor – have also been known to prove impenetrable. To try and help make the gist of the words more accessible to speakers of other varieties of English, here is an 'international' version which will hopefully explain all.

> Wheear 'as tha been sin' ah saw thee?
> On Ilkla Moor baht 'at,
> Wheear 'as tha been sin' ah saw thee?
> Wheear 'as tha been sin' ah saw thee?
> On Ilkla Moor baht 'at,
> On Ilkla Moor baht 'at,
> On Ilkla Moor baht at.
>
> But what do all these strange words mean –
> 'On Ilkla Moor baht 'at'?
> But what do all these strange words mean?
> But what do all these strange words mean?
> On Ilkla Moor baht 'at,
> On Ilkla Moor baht 'at,
> On Ilkla Moor baht at.
>
> They mean your titfer has vamoosed.
> On Ilkla Moor baht 'at.
> They mean your titfer has vamoosed.
> They mean your titfer has vamoosed.
> On Ilkla Moor baht 'at,
> On Ilkla Moor baht 'at,
> On Ilkla Moor baht at.

They mean your chapeau's gone AWOL.
On Ilkla Moor baht 'at.
They mean your chapeau's gone AWOL.
They mean your chapeau's gone AWOL.
On Ilkla Moor baht 'at,
On Ilkla Moor baht 'at,
On Ilkla Moor baht at.

They mean your bonce is in the buff.
On Ilkla Moor baht 'at.
They mean your bonce is in the buff.
They mean your bonce is in the buff.
On Ilkla Moor baht 'at,
On Ilkla Moor baht 'at,
On Ilkla Moor baht at.

So now I hope you understand
'On Ilkla Moor baht 'at'.
So now I hope you understand.
So now I hope you understand.
Since we last 'ad a chat,
You've gorn 'n lost yer 'at
On Ilkla Moor Baht 'at!

Week Ending

As well as providing a weekly bedtime helping of fairly gentle satire, the now long-defunct Radio 4 show *Week Ending* also offered aspiring comedy writers one of the few routes available to get their gags aired on BBC radio. Some weeks, the writing credits list seemed to go on longer than many of the sketches. Here are few of my own submissions to the programme.

> A big shake-up has been announced at the Met. Office. There is now a separate department for rain and showers, one for sleet and snow, and one for damp and drizzle. The Met. Office itself will just act as an umbrella organisation.

> A Church of England vicar has caused a storm by announcing plans to marry for the seventh time. In the village of Much Poking, his latest engagement to the lady behind the counter at the post-office has shocked parishioners. Churchwarden Miss Ethel Goodbody today said 'It's disgusting. Everyone in the village knows it was my turn next.'

> After the claim by the chairman of PowerGen that UK electricity prices are the cheapest in Europe, cross-channel ferries from Calais have been packed with French day-trippers carrying electric kettles, heaters and food mixers. A Frenchman with three vacuum cleaners said he hoping to clean up in the south of England.

> There was a fresh controversy this week over the use of artificial football pitches when a new survey by the FA revealed that the most successful teams always win on aggregate.

The current World Scrabble-playing champion, Jonquil K Xylophone, recently completed another record-breaking marathon game. He described the event to reporters as a 'zigzagging juxtaposition of quixotic ambidexterity' for which he was awarded a total of 853 points.

Bangkok students who were caught with radio receivers in their underwear during an army entrance exam claim they had simply misunderstood a TV commercial which promised that their whites would be so much brighter with Aerial power.

Following reports of a massive fossil drain from the UK, Scotland Yard have placed a round-the-clock guard on the homes of Bruce Forsyth, Mick Jagger and Cliff Richard.

The latest TUC campaign to boost the wages of Britain's part-time workers has won the backing of the Institute of Company Directors. An Institute spokesman revealed that some of their members received as little as £85,000 a year for their two half-days' work a month.

Steam Radio

Steam Radio is a one-act play set in a radio studio in the not-so-distant past just prior to the broadcast of 'Shortish Encounter' – any passing resemblance to a certain steamy film written by Sir Noël Coward is entirely unaccidental! Inevitably, things don't go entirely as planned…

CHARACTERS (and, where applicable, their parts in the radio play)

HERMIONE	(Laura Johnson)
GEORGE	(Dr Alec Harley; Fred – Laura's husband)
ROSE	(Mrs Bassett – the refreshment room manageress)
MAURICE	(Mr Perkins – the ticket inspector)
SUZANNE	(Iris – the waitress; Dulcie – Laura's friend; Tommy – Laura's son)
RICHARD	Studio director
TERRY	Studio sound engineer
CLEANER	Studio cleaner

HERMIONE and GEORGE are seasoned 'old-school' actors, long-sufferingly married.
ROSE is a fairly extrovert type, and a chum of HERMIONE.
MAURICE is gay and, with suitable encouragement, can be quite camp. In contrast to his radio play rôle, he is not at all cockney.
SUZANNE is attractive, somewhat emotional, and not long out of drama school.
RICHARD is rather pretentious and bombastic, and not overly competent.
TERRY is a hi-fi and train-spotting enthusiast.
CLEANER is the archetypal charwoman.

HERMIONE and GEORGE are in their fifties, and SUZANNE in her early twenties. The ages of the other characters are fairly flexible. TERRY could possibly be played as a woman's part. The cast and the radio parts they play should be as vocally distinct as possible, for example Suzanne might, herself, have a Liverpool accent.

There are several chairs, a small table, a wooden cupboard, and a metal wastepaper bin. Downstage are three microphones on stands which the actors use when performing the radio play. At the back of the studio there is a prominent panel with separate illuminated signs for ON THE AIR and REHEARSAL.

Separated from the main studio area by a (possibly imaginary or implied) windowed (but actually glassless) partition, running upstage-downstage, is the small control room. At the upstage end of the partition is some kind of connecting door or curtain through to the studio – this could be in the partition itself, or via a short backstage route. At the downstage end is a large reel-to-reel tape deck, a rack of tapes, some kind of simple mixing desk, a telephone etc. There is a microphone on the desk, through which the control room can talk to the main studio when required. Ideally, the control room microphone should be practical and slightly amplified. The tape-deck, on the other hand, will not actually be the source of the sound effects heard during the play. On the wall is a large clock, side-on to the audience so the hands cannot clearly be seen.

Depending on the studio and control room props being used, the play may be set at any more or less any time between the 1950s and the 1990s. References to the BBC Home Service *should be read as* BBC Radio 4 *if the setting is post-1967. Similarly, the final pip of the Greenwich time-pips was lengthened in the mid-1970s. With a more recent setting, mineral-water might be a more appropriate substitute for the lemonade that features in the play.*

Initially, the stage is in darkness. We hear the sound of a loud express steam-train passing through a station blowing its whistle, followed by the stirring opening of Rachmaninov's Second Piano Concerto. As the music fades we hear another train pulling out of the station over which there is an announcement on the station Tannoy.

TANNOY   Milton Junction – Milton Junction. The next train to arrive at platform one will be the 5.38 for Chelford.

As the train noise fades, the stage lights, including the REHEARSAL sign, slowly come up. In the control room, the tape deck is in motion. It is operated by TERRY who is wearing headphones. When the train sound has all but disappeared, RICHARD, who is holding a stop-watch and a script in a binder, signals first to TERRY who stops the tape, then signals through the window for ROSE to begin. ROSE is using the microphone farthest from the control room, MAURICE is at the centre.

ROSE   So I said to him, I think you'll find those rock buns were fresh this morning.

MAURICE   Gerraway.

ROSE   And if *he* had any ideas about getting fresh, I'd give him more than he'd bargained for!

MAURICE   Lawks a mercy, Mrs Bassett, you never did, did you?

ROSE   I did indeed, Mr Perkins. Ooh, you should have seen his face. If looks could kill...

MAURICE   Well you certainly know how to handle men, Mrs Bassett, and no mistake.

ROSE   I know not what to what you are alluding to, I'm sure, Mr Perkins. Of course, you got a *much* better class of traveller before the war. Much more refined. Real gentlemen – not unlike yourself, if you'll pardon my familiarity. And what are you doing standing there with your ears flapping, Iris? Table three needs clearing – if it's not too much trouble, of course.

SUZANNE, who has apparently been engrossed in filing her nails up to this point, ambles up to the microphone with perfect timing to deliver her line.

SUZANNE   (*As IRIS*) Yes, Mrs Bassett.

RICHARD signals to TERRY who presses a button on the tape deck and the spools start revolving. We hear the sounds of cups and saucers being clinked. SUZANNE ambles back upstage, still engrossed in her nails. GEORGE gives her a conspiratorial wink.

ROSE   And of course, you can't get the staff these days either.

MAURICE   I know exactly what you mean, Mrs Bassett. That new porter on the morning shift – he's just the same. The younger generation, tch.

RICHARD signals again to TERRY who fades the crockery sound then stops the tape. Towards the end of the next speech, MAURICE gradually and very smoothly turns away from his microphone – illustrating an audio fade-out effect. GEORGE performs the reverse manoeuvre, with a slight overlap, to give a fade-in effect.

MAURICE	'Ere, I had a right one this morning. Chap with a third class ticket on the 9.15 was in the lavatory and pulled the bloomin' communication cord. Swore blind he'd meant to pull the lavatory chain. So, I told him straight, if the train was in the station, either way it was against regulations. But would he have it? In the end, I had to send for Mr Hancock – and you can imagine what Mr Hancock had to say...
GEORGE	*(As ALEC)* Laura! Laura! So there you are. Oh Laura, darling, I've been looking for you everywhere. Thank God I've found you at last. When you ran away like that I felt so awfully beastly. I started to imagine all sorts of ghastly things had happened to you.

HERMIONE joins GEORGE at the centre microphone.

HERMIONE	Alec. It's no good. I just had to get away from that awful flat. I just don't know how we got into all this.
GEORGE	Oh Laura, you mean so much to me.
HERMIONE	Oh Alec, you know that I love you with all my being. I've never been happier than in these past few months with all the time we've spent together. But if we look in our hearts, I think that deep down we both know that it could never be. We have our own lives and our own responsibilities. I have to think of my children, Tommy and Dorothy, and Trixie the dog, and the guinea-pigs Flopsy and Mopsy, and the goldfish. And of course there's my husband Fred. Dear, ordinary, reliable, conventional, respectable, decent, stiff upper-lipped, boring, tedious old Fred.

During the next speech, HERMIONE starts brushing fluff off GEORGE's shoulder in a proprietorial way. She finds a long hair and suspiciously hold it aloft. GEORGE is slightly thrown for moment.

GEORGE	I can hardly remember the time before you came into my life. You know, Laura, when I'm not with you the days pass so slowly, and life just seems so grey and empty

and meaningless. I just don't know how much longer I can go on like this. Oh, if only I'd met you years ago – who knows how things might have turned out. But now, it's all getting so complicated. I think my wife (*He tries to grab the hair from HERMIONE but fails then scowls at her*) is starting to suspect something.

HERMIONE   It was bound to happen eventually.

GEORGE   Oh, it seems so unfair, dash it all. Laura, my dear...

HERMIONE   Yes, darling?

GEORGE   There's something I have to tell you. I've been putting it off all day but it simply can't wait any longer. You see the thing is, I've been offered a new job. As a senior doctor in a new hospital in Africa.

HERMIONE   Oh Alec, I feel so stupid. I wish I understood all those complicated medical words. But we must be brave. And you know Alec, deep down I think we both know it could never have worked. Love's all very well, but what about self-respect and decency and stiff upper lips? Oh darling, what are we going to do?

GEORGE   Oh, darling we have so little time.

HERMIONE   Alec, could you light me a cigarette?

GEORGE   Of course, darling.

RICHARD and TERRY repeat their routine with the tape and we hear the amplified sound of a cigarette lighter.

GEORGE   You know I always think of you when I use this lighter that you gave me.

During SUZANNE's next speech (at the microphone nearest the control room), HERMIONE looks at SUZANNE's hair, then at the hair which she is still holding – we can see the wheels going round inside her head. SUZANNE is momentarily thrown but pretends not to notice.

SUZANNE   (*As the garrulous DULCIE*) Hello there Laura. Fancy seeing you here! Oh, I'm sorry, you're with someone. Look do you mind if put these bags down – I've shopped

	till I've flopped. I was browsing around the linen department in Shackleton's – they always have such lovely towels don't you think, especially that pastel pink. And their towels are so soft and fluffy. When you drape yourself in one after a hot bath and feel its silky texture gently caressing your bare buttocks and thighs... and they come up so well in the wash. The towels, that is, of course. Well Laura, you mustn't let me chatter on like this – aren't you going to introduce me to your friend? Hello, I'm Dulcie Pargeter.
HERMIONE	Dulcie, this is Dr Harley.
GEORGE	Alec. Hello.
SUZANNE	I say, would you mind most awfully getting me a cup of tea. I'm feeling a little...
RICHARD	(*Via the speaker from the control room*) Hold on everyone. George lovey, absolutely tremendous performance darling, but that last line of yours.
GEORGE	You mean 'Alec. Hello?'
RICHARD	Yes dear boy, well it's that 'hello.' I'm wondering if we could do a bit more with it? Possibly convey something more of Alec's essential ambivalence to the situation in which he finds himself, his primordial but unrequited yearning for his beloved Laura, his fundamental humanity as a committed member of the medical profession, his frustration at the unexpected arrival of the interloper...
HERMIONE	(*Acidly*) The fact that he's old enough to be her father.

GEORGE glares at her.

GEORGE	Thank you Hermione, dear. By the way darling, I've been meaning to ask you – is that a new hair-do?
HERMIONE	Why, yes George. I was wondering if you'd noticed.
GEORGE	Well, I know it's half price for pensioners on Tuesdays. OK Richard, I'll see what I can do.

RICHARD	All right, everyone. Top of page six. OK Terry? *(TERRY gives a nod)* Can you give him the cue, Hermione.
HERMIONE	Dulcie, this is Dr Harley.
GEORGE	Alec. Helloooohh.

SUZANNE smiles at GEORGE and mimes applause. He gives her a smug smile back. HERMIONE snorts.

SUZANNE	I say, would you mind most awfully getting me a cup of tea. I'm feeling a little…

There is a pause. Everyone looks expectantly at GEORGE whose line it now is. He is still making eyes at SUZANNE.

GEORGE	What? Oh, is it me. Sorry. Er, I hadn't realised you wanted us to carry on, Richard. Was that all right by the way? Primordial enough for you? *(GEORGE winks at SUZANNE)*
RICHARD	Ravishing, lovey.

HERMIONE mimes puking to MAURICE. She catches GEORGE looking at her and feigns a cough.

MAURICE	Ooh, that's a nasty cough you've got there, Hermione. I hope it's not going around. I think I felt a bit of a tickle in the bathroom this morning.
RICHARD	OK boys and girls. Terry? Right, once more, and straight on this time.
HERMIONE	Dulcie, this is Dr Harley.
GEORGE	Alec. Hellooooooooooooooouuuuhh.

HERMIONE raises her eyebrows.

SUZANNE	I say, would you mind most awfully getting me a cup of tea. I'm feeling a little…

Having overdone his line, GEORGE has developed a coughing fit.

HERMIONE	I think you'd be quicker making the tea yourself, dear.
MAURICE	*(Into one of the microphones)* Talking of tea, I hope we get a break before transmission. I'm gasping back here.

RICHARD   All right everyone, I don't think we've got time to go any further with that. Could we just have a quick canter through the flashback scene on page fifteen? OK, Hermione? All right Terry – whenever you're ready.

HERMIONE and GEORGE are standing at different microphones. TERRY starts the tape and we hear the sound of a car engine which rapidly fades at the appropriate point.

HERMIONE   We were out in the country and were feeling quite jolly. We'd had a delightful lunch in the cafeteria at the hospital where Alec works – steamed fish, boiled potatoes and cauliflower, followed by a scrummy tapioca pudding. Then Alec said he'd take the afternoon off as he hadn't much else to do that day – just an open heart operation and a couple of kidney transplants. Oh, I wish I understood all those complicated medical words. So, there we were, bowling along a country lane in Alec's car when, suddenly, we pulled over at the side of the road. Alec looked across at me with his big brown eyes and said...

GEORGE   Darling, there's something I just have to get off my chest. It's completely absurd I know but, now that it's happened, I think it's only fair to both of us to face up to it. Oh, Laura, my darling...

HERMIONE   Yes, Alec? What is it you're trying to tell me?

GEORGE   Oh, Laura – my life, my love...

HERMIONE   Yes, Alec, yes...

GEORGE   I... I... I think we've run out of petrol.

HERMIONE   Oh, Alec – I don't give two hoots about the car.

            And with that, he enfolded me in his strong arms and – our lips finally met!

MAURICE, standing at GEORGE's microphone, sucks the back of his hand to produce deliberately exaggerated kissing noises. GEORGE puts on a pained expression.

	Of course, I was frightfully late getting home that evening, and as I walked in the front door, Fred was there waiting for me.
GEORGE	*(As FRED)* I say, Laura, thank goodness you're here. Tommy's been refusing to go to sleep till you got home.
SUZANNE	*(As TOMMY)* Mummy, Mummy – Flopsy and Mopsy escaped from their cage and Trixie was chasing them all around the garden. Then I was chasing Trixie, and Daddy was chasing me. *(She smirks at GEORGE)* It was jolly wizard fun! Oh, I do wish you'd been here to see Daddy chasing me round the garden, Mummy.
HERMIONE	So do I, Tommy, so do I.
GEORGE	*(Leering across at SUZANNE)* Right Tommy, come along now. I want to see you tucked up in bed ready for your goodnight kiss.

MAURICE looks at GEORGE, then SUZANNE, then back to GEORGE, giving him a knowing look.

RICHARD	*(Via the control-room microphone)* OK, thank you everyone. I think we're going to have to leave it there. You're all doing marvellously well. There's less than fifteen minutes before we go on the air, so don't go too far away.

TERRY flicks a switch and the REHEARSAL light goes out.

SUZANNE	I think I'll just pop down to the canteen. Can I get anyone anything?
HERMIONE	*(To ROSE)* A decent co-star.
GEORGE	What was that, darling?
HERMIONE	A fruit and nut bar. *(Patronizingly)* Why, my dear child, how very kind of you to offer. I'm sure I don't deserve it. Some tea would be very nice, please. Darjeeling if they have it.
SUZANNE	Right. One tea.

HERMIONE	*(Trying to be difficult)* In a nice white china cup and saucer. I can't stand those awful mugs everyone uses these days. The tea just doesn't taste the same.
SUZANNE	Right. One tea, white china.
HERMIONE	Oh, and could you possibly ask them for a left-handed cup. Er, my arthritis, you know. But of course you mustn't put yourself to any trouble on my account.
SUZANNE	*(Sweetly)* I wouldn't dream of such a thing. I'll see if they've got a left-handed spoon as well, shall I? What about you, Maurice?
MAURICE	Ooh, I could murder a gin and tonic but I suppose Sir would kick up a fuss. I'll just have a milky coffee, please dear.
ROSE	Well, I'm feeling extravagant today. Could you get me some cheese-and-onion crisps and a lemonade?
SUZANNE	OK. Anyone else? *(She moves to the control-room window and makes a cup-rocking gesture)*
RICHARD	*(Via the control-room microphone)* I think we're amply provided for in here, thank you, darling. Terry has kindly brought along a large thermos-flask and a bounteous supply of fish-paste sandwiches of which I have been munificently asked to partake.
SUZANNE	Right then – one tea, one coffee, one lemonade, one cheese-and-onion.
HERMIONE	What an obliging little thing you are, dear. Isn't she, George?
GEORGE	You must let me come and help you, Suzanne.
SUZANNE	Why, thank you kind sir.
GEORGE	It'll be my pleasure. And on the way we can have a quick chat about one or two aspects of your part – a bit of fatherly guidance from an old hand. Besides, it's suddenly got very stuffy in here.
SUZANNE	Right, shan't be long.

SUZANNE and GEORGE exit. MAURICE sits down and reads a copy of The Stage. *In the control room, RICHARD is making notes on his script. TERRY is rewinding the tape.*

ROSE — Fatherly guidance indeed! And I know which aspects of her parts that his old hands are interested in.

HERMIONE — You don't have to tell me dear. I've been married to George for nearly fifteen years, remember. I know all about his slimy little ways. In fact, I can probably tell you exactly what he's saying to Suzanne at this very minute. *(She starts mimicking George)* It's quite clear to me that you have a very special gift, m'dear. Yours is a talent that, with the right kind of nurturing – from the right person, could take you to the top of our profession. Of course, I knew it from the very first moment I laid eyes on you...

HERMIONE/ROSE *(Together, making the same exaggerated dramatic gesture)* A bright new star in the thespian firmament. *(They laugh)*

MAURICE — Did I miss something?

HERMIONE — No Maurice. Just an old joke, a *very* old joke. *(To ROSE)* It's nothing to laugh at really, though. Whenever George feels the sap rising and starts chasing after some femme fatale, it's always me who suffers. If he gets rejected, then he's impossible for weeks. And if he doesn't get the elbow, then he's even *more* insufferable. You know, Rose, I think he honestly believes I swallow all those pathetic stories he comes out with.

ROSE — Well, I suppose he's at that awkward age.

HERMIONE — He's been at that awkward age for the last twelve years. I sometimes think I've just about had enough.

ROSE — Come on, it's not that bad. He just likes to flirt, that's all.

HERMIONE — Perhaps. But one of these days, he may just push his luck a little bit too far. Anyway, how are things with you, Maurice? Any good auditions coming up?

MAURICE Well, I thought this one here sounded rather up my street...

ROSE and HERMIONE gather round MAURICE to look at his paper. Over in the control room, RICHARD has been studying his stop-watch and script.

RICHARD Terry, it still looks like we're over-running a smidgen. I think we need to save about twenty seconds somewhere. Any bright ideas?

TERRY Well, there is that train sequence on page 19. We've been using a standard recording out of the sound library. It's a Castle class 4-6-0 loco on that uphill stretch of the Sheffield and District Railway Company's line to Barnsley before it was re-laid in 1946. So although it's roughly the right vintage traction-wise, it's completely the wrong track acoustic. Any spotter worth his salt would notice it a mile off, of course. I shouldn't be surprised if the BBC switchboard was jammed with complaints.

RICHARD Really Terry, that's absolutely fascinating, but...

TERRY Now I do happen to have with me a recording I made myself of a restored Midland Class 4-4-0 pulling mixed freight on a mid-week afternoon past platform four at Carnforth station.

RICHARD That really is most interesting Terry, but could we get to the...

TERRY Right stock, right location, and most important of all for our purposes... *(RICHARD looks hopefully at TERRY)* ... superb tonal ambience.

RICHARD Terry, dear heart, do you think that by any remote possibility you could just give me a...

TERRY And, of course, it'd save you seventeen and a half seconds...

RICHARD ... just give me a chance to make a note of that. Platform four you say...

Meanwhile, MAURICE, HERMIONE and ROSE have been looking at audition notices.

MAURICE I don't know what you mean Rose, I've always rather fancied myself in Lincoln Green.

HERMIONE If you ask me, it's any excuse to wear tights with you, Maurice. No matter what the colour.

ROSE By the way, Maurice, I've been meaning to ask you – you're not still seeing that nice boy from the TV make-up department by any chance?

MAURICE Russell, you mean? Well, he fits me in once in a while – if you know what I mean. He's very much in demand though, is Russell – professionally speaking of course. Wouldn't have thought he was your type, Rose.

ROSE Well I was wondering if there's any chance he could get me some more of that French lipstick. You know the stuff I mean, waterproof, windproof and... kiss-proof.

MAURICE No probs, dear. Can't say it's ever worked for me though. Not once Russell's got the bit between his teeth. Actually, I may even have a couple in my bag. Remind me to have a rummage for you when we've wrapped up here. If my memory serves me right, there's a very nice misty peach that'd probably suit you.

TERRY *(Wearing headphones, via the control room microphone)* Rose, can you spare a mo? That microphone at the far side's been cutting in and out a bit. You wouldn't like to test it for me, would you?

ROSE For you darling, anything. Now what would you like? I could do you the cocktail-party scene from King Lear. Or how about the tap-dancing sequence from Hedda Gabler? Or that big Act 2 chorus number from Waiting for Godot. I know – there's that voice-over job I did last week for ITV – 'Mother always said that a way to man's heart is through his stomach. And you know, she was right. So ask your newsagent for Surgery for Beginners,

	out now in twenty-six weekly parts. Get a free kidney-bowl with part one.'
TERRY	(*Twiddling knobs and looking puzzled*) It's still not right. Sounds like it might be a dodgy electrolytic cardioid coupler. Could you just give me a bit more?
ROSE	(*Going into a Gracie Fields impersonation*) Eeeh, you're never satisfied, young fella. Me mother always warned me about lads likes you. (*She starts to sing, ending on a very loud high note*) Oh Walter, Walter, lead me to the altar. You're more than the whole world to me!
TERRY	(*Removing headphones*) She's blown it completely now. I'll have to nip down to the stores to get a replacement.

TERRY *exits to the main studio and starts to disconnect the faulty microphone.*

RICHARD	(*Calling after him*) You'd better get your skates on. We're on the air in less than ten minutes.
TERRY	(*Looking at his watch*) Eight minutes, twenty-three seconds.

RICHARD *puts on the headphones. MAURICE goes over to TERRY and looks at him smoulderingly.*

MAURICE	Oh, You're a quick worker, aren't you Terry. I've heard all about you, you know. Is it true you've got the biggest pair of woofers this side of Watford? Ooh, you can come and twiddle my knobs any time you like, dear. Actually, if you're not doing anything after the show, I could take you to this bijou little bar I know.
ROSE	You don't mean to the Goat and Anorak. Well now, there's an offer.

TERRY *exits rapidly.*

HERMIONE	Now, now, you two. By the way, Rose, I should put in for a bonus if were you. Aren't they supposed to pay a higher rate for singing?

ROSE   Not on this production, they don't. It's low-budget, in case you hadn't noticed. That's why it's going out live – to save on studio time. And why George and Suzanne are both playing more than one part.

HERMIONE   Well, if you want my opinion, that's probably a little arrangement that George cooked up with Uncle Dickie over there. No doubt so he could have an excuse for some extra rehearsals.

ROSE   Private ones, of course.

HERMIONE   Very private, if the state of George's collars the past few days are anything to go by.

RICHARD   *(Via the control room microphone)* I didn't hear my name being taken in vain just then, did I Hermione?

HERMIONE   *(Moving to one of the studio microphones)* I can't think what you mean, dear boy. *(She deliberately taps on the microphone with her finger, deafening RICHARD)* Is this mike OK, by the way?

ROSE   Oh well, I suppose one should be grateful for working at all these days. Particularly when you get to our age.

HERMIONE   *(Returning to ROSE and MAURICE)* Oh, grateful doesn't enter into, Rose. It's a disgrace how few roles there are for, well, the more mature actress. It's just so topsy-turvy – the more experienced we get, the fewer parts there are for us to play. And what ones there are usually get given to the likes of what's-her-face. Even on radio, where you all you use is the voice, you'd sometimes think that the size of your bust was the main qualification for getting a part.

ROSE   I know dear. You'd think it would work the other way round wouldn't you? I mean, a big bust stops you getting close up to the mike. *(They laugh)* Oh, I've just remembered – there's something I need to have a little chat with Richard about. *(She goes over into the control room)* Dickie-Dums...

RICHARD	Ah Rose – fair of face, charming of countenance, delicate of demeanour, most modest of maidens, and light of my life. Look, if it's about that money you lent me...
ROSE	No Dickie-Dums, it's not about the money. I gave up all hope of seeing that again, months ago. It's something...
RICHARD	Well, that's remarkably decent...
ROSE	Look, Dickie, would you mind awfully not interrupting for a minute?
RICHARD	Oh right, yes, of course... sorry.
ROSE	Well, the thing is, old son... *(Confidentially)* It's Hermione. You see, she's having a bit of a hard time of things at the moment, one way and another. And I know you're just about to start casting for that broadcast of Romeo and Juliet next month.
RICHARD	Yes, but that's ...

ROSE silences him by raising an index finger.

ROSE	So I wondered, as an extra special favour to me, if you could see your way to giving her a part.
RICHARD	My darling Rose, is *that* all? Absolutely no problem whatsoever. In fact, I'd already been thinking about her for Lady Capulet.
ROSE	No Dickie, not Lady Capulet.
RICHARD	Not Lady Capulet. No. Oh, I see. Well, as it's you Rose, I suppose I could stretch things and offer her the nurse. I can't really see there being a problem...
ROSE	No, not the nurse, not Lady Capulet, nor Lady Montague, nor even the fair Rosaline.
RICHARD	But that only leaves...
ROSE	Yes, Dickie-Dums?
RICHARD	Surely, you can't seriously be proposing that I cast Hermione as...
ROSE	And why not? Oh, look Dickie. It's been her lifelong ambition. And it would really cheer her up.

RICHARD　　But Juliet's barely fourteen. Hermione's... well, Hermione's old enough to be her mother. Her grandmother even.

ROSE　　Is it, or is it not, you who always says that the wireless is superior to the cinema or television – because the pictures are so much better. It's what people hear and imagine that's important. She could do it brilliantly.

RICHARD　　Well, yes, but...

ROSE　　Well, there you are then, it's settled.

RICHARD　　But Rose, I've already half-promised the part of Juliet to...

ROSE　　Then you can jolly well unpromise it. Besides, if you don't...

RICHARD　　Oh dear, you've got that look in your eye.

ROSE　　If you don't, then certain people in high places will finally get to hear the truth about some highly embarrassing, and so far unexplained, little incidents. Like that time we did *Gaslight*. Only, *you* said it would help to create the right atmosphere if we had some cylinders of real gas hissing away. But, of course, for safety reasons, the gas we had to use was helium. Then everyone breathed in the stuff and we all came out sounding like Donald Duck.

RICHARD　　It could have happened to anyone. Besides, Donald Duck's very popular.

ROSE　　Yes, but in a melodrama? Then, of course, there was your infamous production of Snow White? Why you had to use real dwarves is beyond me...

RICHARD　　It was a simple misunderstanding with the agency.

ROSE　　All the microphone stands were too tall and they had to stand on those cardboard boxes which kept collapsing at vital moments. 'Hi-ho, hi-ho, it's arrghhh...' Or there was that other memorable occasion when we were doing *The Jungle Book*...

RICHARD   Oh, Rose, dear heart, you wouldn't...

ROSE   And you let that friend of yours from the safari park talk you into having a real tiger in the studio...

RICHARD   No, please, that was years ago. Look, I'll do anything...

ROSE   And when it proceeded to chew through all those wires, the BBC and half of the West End was blacked out for three hours. Not to mention the shock it gave to the poor tiger. Talk about fur flying. I'm sure the police, the electricity board and the RSPCA would all be very interested in the details on that one.

RICHARD   All right, you win. You're quite right, Rose. Now I've thought about it, I can see it would be absolutely criminal to give Juliet to anyone else other than Hermione.

ROSE   Oh, thank you, dear sweet Dickie-Dums. *(She kisses him on the cheek)* And not a word to anyone, all right? You know I'll do the same for you one day. Ah, I think the troops are back at last.

Enter SUZANNE, carrying a tray, with GEORGE. The tray contains three mugs, three teaspoons heaped with sugar, a small teapot, a tea-strainer with a drip-tray, a tall glass of lemonade with a straw, and a packet of crisps.

GEORGE   Of course, I knew it from the very first moment I laid eyes on you – a bright new star in the thespian firmament.

MAURICE laughs.

GEORGE   Something amusing, dear boy?

MAURICE   Er, no. Just a joke someone was telling me about. I think I've just worked it out.

SUZANNE puts the tray on the table. ROSE comes back into the main studio.

SUZANNE   Sorry we took so long. George insisted on taking a short cut and we somehow ended up in a broom-cupboard. I think we managed to remember everything though. Oh, except the fruit and nut bar, Hermione. I was going to

	get you some ordinary milk chocolate but George said you wanted to lose a bit of weight at the moment, so I thought I'd better leave it.
HERMIONE	Did he now? Well, I suppose I do have this large useless lump I'd be much better off without.

SUZANNE smiles politely, not sure if she understands this remark. She hands GEORGE one of the mugs.

GEORGE	Did you put sugar in mine?
SUZANNE	It's in the spoon.
GEORGE	Of course, you're sweet enough already, Suzanne.

HERMIONE gives GEORGE a dirty look.

HERMIONE	*(So that everyone can hear)* So, Maurice, it's not serious with you and Russell then. I mean, you're not thinking of moving in together or anything drastic?
MAURICE	No…
HERMIONE	Well, if you want my advice, think about it very carefully first. You want to make sure you know all about a man before you take a big step like that.
MAURICE	Is that right?
HERMIONE	Otherwise, you might be in for all sorts of nasty surprises.

HERMIONE looks over at GEORGE who is having a cosy tête-à-tête with SUZANNE.

HERMIONE	Like him shoving his dirty underpants under the bed.
ROSE	Or snoring.
HERMIONE	Or grinding his teeth, eugghhh!
ROSE	Or never helping with the cleaning.
HERMIONE	Especially in the bathroom – must think the toilet magically cleans itself.
ROSE	Or never, ever, cooking a meal.
HERMIONE	Though he can tell you to the exact second how long he likes his eggs boiled for.

By now, GEORGE has realised what is going on and adopts a martyred expression.

HERMIONE   And then you discover that he dyes his hair.

ROSE   Or even worse...

HERMIONE/ROSE/MAURICE   *(Together)* That he wears a wig!

GEORGE protests vehemently to SUZANNE that he does not wear a wig. The phone in the control room rings and is answered by RICHARD.

RICHARD   Yes? That's right. What? What do you mean, stuck? He can't be. But we're just about to go on the air. Can't we wait till they...? Oh, I see. Oh, very well.

RICHARD puts the phone down and comes into the studio.

RICHARD   Look everyone, slight hitch I'm afraid. There seems to be a fault with one of the lifts. It's got itself stuck between the second and third floors.

HERMIONE   But it's always doing that. I generally take the stairs these days. So what's the problem?

RICHARD   The problem, Hermione darling, is that not only is the lift stuck, but that our entire technical department, namely Terry, is incarcerated inside the wretched thing and there's no knowing how long it may be before they get it fixed. And, in case you hadn't noticed, we are due on air with a live drama production in a little under three minutes time.

SUZANNE   But can't some else do all the technical thingummy-jiggery?

RICHARD   Oh would that it were that simple, Suzanne my love. Apart from the fact that the technicians union would close down the entire BBC if a non-union member should dare so much as to move a microphone, the cues for all the various tapes et cetera are in Terry's charming but indecipherable scrawl on the back of this bus ticket. *(He unfurls a long bus ticket)*. On the other hand, I have it on *very* good authority that a certain senior member of the Royal Family is an avid fan of our modest efforts and is almost certainly at this very moment snuggling up in front of the wireless with a hot milk and whisky. If we don't dig ourselves out of this mess, we could all find ourselves blacklisted from these hallowed portals for a very long time to come. I propose, therefore, that after due and careful consideration of all the options open to us, and given the fact we're on the air in less than *two* minutes, we sod the bloody technicians union and do the best we can without them. I shall endeavour to do what I can with the infernal tape machine. I suggest that the rest of you, for once, try to act like professionals *(everyone looks daggers at him)* and improvise using whatever resources we have at our disposal to get this damn show on the road!

SUZANNE starts clapping in admiration at RICHARD's speech but stops suddenly when she realises that no-one else is joining in.

GEORGE	What resources?
RICHARD	I beg your pardon, George?
GEORGE	I said, what resources?
RICHARD	Well, there's a few odds and ends around the place. Table and chairs and so on. And I think there's some bits and pieces in that cupboard over there. What else do you need? Didn't they teach you anything at drama school? *(GEORGE looks as if he might kill RICHARD at any moment. RICHARD looks around at everyone then goes into WW2 Squadron-Leader mode)* Look everyone, I just wanted to say – you're pretty well the finest body of men, and women, it's been my privilege to know. Now, we've got a job of work to do and, by jingo, I know you won't let me down... *(He grabs an umbrella and starts waving it like a sword.)*
	The game's afoot
	Follow your spirit; and, upon this charge
	Cry 'God for Harry! England and Saint George!'

RICHARD raises the umbrella in salute, tosses it to the floor, and strides back into the control room. The others look at each other in stunned silence.

ROSE   Well, come on – let's get ourselves organised!

Everyone starts scrabbling for their scripts, and turning out the cupboard contents into a heap on the floor. RICHARD meanwhile has put on the headphones and is trying to operate the tape deck – we hear high-pitched gobbledy-gook as the tape goes backwards and forwards.

RICHARD   OK everyone, ten seconds.

A couple of seconds later we hear the Greenwich time-pips.

RICHARD   This is the BBC Home Service. It's 8 o'clock and time for the final part of our Tuesday serial, *Shortish Encounter* by Cole Howard, starring George Fielding as Alec, and Hermione Fielding as Laura. *Shortish Encounter.*

RICHARD starts the tape deck. We hear a loud express steam-train passing through a station, blowing its whistle. MAURICE gives RICHARD a thumbs-up. We then hear a blast of a loud rock-and-roll song. RICHARD fast-forwards the tape. We hear a snatch of Scottish country dancing music, then finally the correct sound of another train pulling out of the station. RICHARD gestures wildly at MAURICE who points to himself and mimes the word 'Me?'.

MAURICE   Oh, right – I'm with you. *(Holding his nose between his fingers)* Milton Junction – Milton Junction. The next train to arrive at platform one will be the 5.38 for Chelford.

ROSE   So I said to him, I think you'll find those rock buns were fresh this morning.

MAURICE   Gerraway.

ROSE   And if *he* had any ideas about getting fresh, I'd give him more than he'd bargained for!

MAURICE   Lawks a mercy, Mrs Bassett, you never did, did you?

ROSE   I did indeed, Mr Perkins. Ooh, you should have seen his face. If looks could kill...

MAURICE   Well, you certainly know how to handle men, Mrs Bassett, and no mistake.

ROSE   I know not what to what you are alluding to, I'm sure, Mr Perkins. Of course, you got a *much* better class of traveller before the war. Much more refined. Real gentlemen – not unlike yourself, if you'll pardon my familiarity. And what are you doing standing there with your ears flapping, Iris? Table three needs clearing – if it's not too much trouble, of course.

SUZANNE   Yes, Mrs Bassett.

RICHARD is having trouble with the tape for the next sound effect. SUZANNE looks around for something with which to make the sounds of the crockery. She gets a mug and a glass of lemonade from the canteen tray and starts loudly tapping them together very close to one of the microphones. The others try to make suitable background mumbling noises. RICHARD gives a yell and pulls off his headphones. He waves her back from the microphone. Going back to the tray she spills lemonade everywhere, including GEORGE and HERMIONE's scripts which are lying there.

ROSE   Of course, you can't get the staff these days either.

At the end of the next speech, MAURICE attempts to do his fade-out manoeuvre but collides with GEORGE who, in the mêlée, is fading-in from the wrong side.

MAURICE   I know exactly what you mean, Mrs Bassett. 'Ere, I had a right one this morning. Chap with a third class ticket on the 9.15 was in the lavatory and pulled the bloomin' communication cord. Swore blind he'd meant to pull the lavatory chain. So, I told him straight, if the train was in the station, either way it was against regulations. But would he have it? In the end, I had to send for Mr Hancock – and you can imagine what Mr Hancock had to say...

GEORGE   Can't you look where you're going, you idiot.

MAURICE   *(In character)* Oh no, I don't think Mr Hancock would have said that...

GEORGE and HERMIONE's scripts are dripping wet.

HERMIONE   Laura! Laura! So there you are. Oh Laura, darling, I've been looking for you everywhere. Thank God I've found you at last. When you ran away like that I felt so awfully beastly. I started to imagine all sorts of ghastly things had happened to you.

GEORGE   Oh Alec, you know that I love you with all my being. I've never been happier than in these past few months. But I have to think of my children, Tommy and Dorothy, and Trixie the dog, and the guinea-pigs Flopsy and Mopsy...

HERMIONE and GEORGE finally realise that in the confusion they've picked up each other's scripts. They check the script covers then rapidly swap back.

HERMIONE   *(Deep voice)* As I was saying, there's my husband Fred. Oh dear, I do wish this cold would clear up. *(Clears throat, resumes normal voice)* Ah, that's better. Dear, ordinary, reliable, conventional, respectable, decent, stiff upper-lipped, boring, tedious old Fred.

GEORGE   *(High voice)* Oh Laura, you mean so much... *(Clears throat, resumes normal voice)* you mean so much to me. Oh, if only I'd met you years ago – who knows how things might have turned out. *(HERMIONE has spotted a doodled heart-and-arrow on the back of GEORGE's script – he tries to manoeuvre so she can't see it)* But it's all getting so complicated. I think my wife is starting to suspect something.

HERMIONE   It was bound to happen eventually.

GEORGE   It seems so unfair, dash it all. Laura, my dear...

HERMIONE   Yes, darling?

GEORGE   There's something I have to tell you. You see the thing is, I've been offered a new job. As a senior doctor in a hospital in Africa.

HERMIONE   Oh Alec, I feel so stupid. I wish I understood all those complicated medical words. But we must be... *(She peers at her script)* snake? slave? *(Away from the microphone)*

69

That lemonade's made the ink on my damn script run. I can't make out half the words. Give me yours for a minute, George. Oh *brave*! Silly me. *(She swaps scripts with GEORGE then turns back to the microphone)* But Alec, we must be brave. And you know Alec, deep down I think we both know that it could never have... parked? ... corked? You know George, your script isn't much better than mine. Now, where was I? Oh yes – love's all very well, but what about shelf-respect and degeneracy and stiff copper pipes? Oh daubing, what are we going to dig?

GEORGE Oh Alec, I feel so stupid. I wish I understood all these complicated medical words...

GEORGE realises that he again has the wrong script and exchanges back with HERMIONE.

GEORGE Oh, darling we have so little time.

HERMIONE You took the words right out of my mouth! Oh Alec, could you light me a cigarette?

GEORGE Of course, darling.

He looks desperately around, miming a lighter to everyone. MAURICE and ROSE scrabble in the pile on the floor and find a large box of matches but manage to spill its contents onto the floor. ROSE tries to light a match but fails. She tries another, and another.

ROSE *(Hissing to SUZANNE)* They're all wet.

HERMIONE On second thoughts, perhaps I won't bother.

ROSE finally manages to get a match to light.

GEORGE You know I always think of you when I use this... match that you gave me.

During the next speech MAURICE laboriously picks up the matches scattered around SUZANNE's feet, lifting up her foot to retrieve ones she is standing one. She gamefully carries on but accidentally treads on his hand.

SUZANNE *(As DULCIE)* Hello there Laura. Fancy seeing you here! Do you mind if put these bags down – I've shopped till

	I've flopped. I was browsing around the linen department in Shackleton's – they always have such lovely towels don't you think, especially that pastel pink. And their towels are so soft and fluffy. When you drape yourself in one after a hot bath and feel its silky texture gently caressing your bare buttocks and thighs... and they come up so well in the wash. The towels, that is, of course. Well Laura, you mustn't let me chatter on like this – aren't you going to introduce me to your friend? Hello, I'm Dulcie Pargeter.
HERMIONE	Dulcie, this is Dr Harley.
GEORGE	(*He battles his way to SUZANNE's microphone, sending MAURICE and his collected matches flying*) Alec. (*He takes SUZANNE's hand and gazes at her adoringly.*) Heelloouuh.
SUZANNE	I say, would you mind most awfully getting me a cup of tea. I'm feeling a little queasy...
HERMIONE	(*Aside, to ROSE*) I think we all are, dear.
GEORGE	Of course.

Towards the end of the next speech SUZANNE performs the voice-fade manoeuvre by moving back from the microphone. GEORGE goes to collect a mug from the canteen tray.

SUZANNE	Well, you're a dark horse Laura, where have you been hiding him? He's very attractive, I must say. And a doctor you say, how fascinating. Now you really must let me invite him round to dinner – our garden's looking really lovely at the moment. And last weekend we picked the year's first crop of rhubarb, rhubarb, rhubarb...

SUZANNE intermittently mutters the word 'rhubarb' over the next speech.

HERMIONE	And as Dulcie prattled on, I kept wanting to tell her – shut up you stupid woman. We have so little time left together. Why can't you understand? Oh, why can't you see? (*She stops using the script but stays in character*) You waltz in here, the ink still wet on your Equity card, and

	start making eyes at an ageing has-been who's old enough to be your father. You make sick, young lady. *(The others are now frantically trying to find the right place in the script)* I expect he's given you all those old lines about how you've got a very special talent and how he's prepared to nurture it but, let me tell you, you're not the first one he's had on his casting couch and I'm sure you won't be the last!
SUZANNE	*(Starting to sob)* ... rhubarb, rhubarb, rhubarb.
GEORGE	Here's your tea, Mrs Pargeter. *(He rattles a mug and teaspoon, then 'accidentally' spills some of the cup's contents over HERMIONE)* Oh, I'm so sorry, I seem to have spilt it. How clumsy of me. *(He puts the mug down on the floor)* Never mind – no damage done, eh? Look, here's a hanky. *(He takes a hanky from his pocket. HERMIONE reaches to take it but instead he gives it to SUZANNE to dry her eyes with.)*
SUZANNE	Oh, you're so sweet, George... I mean Doctor Harley. *(She returns to the script)* Er, I was just saying to Laura, you must come round to dinner soon. By the way, have you known Laura long?

The next two pairs of speeches are each spoken simultaneously. GEORGE, who has been fussing over SUZANNE, gets his lines the wrong way around.

HERMIONE	Just a few weeks.
GEORGE	Years and years.
HERMIONE	Years and years.
GEORGE	Just a few weeks.
GEORGE	Well, actually we first met years and years ago.
HERMIONE	But, lost touch. Isn't that right, Alec?
GEORGE	Yes, lost touch completely. But then we met up again, just a few weeks ago. On this very station in fact. You see, Laura got an enormous lump of grit in her eye and I helped her to remove it. *(SUZANNE seems to have something in her eye.)* And you know, I still keep that big

	lump of grit wrapped up in this old hanky of mine. *(He reaches in his pocket for the hanky then realises he has already given it to SUZANNE)* Oh, my God. Suzanne, are you all right. Oh you poor child. Quick someone, send for a doctor.
ROSE	Try pulling your eyelid down as far as it will go.
MAURICE	And then blow your nose.
GEORGE	This is all your fault, Hermione.
SUZANNE	It's all right George, it's just my contact lens.
GEORGE	Oh, I see. Right, sorry everyone. *(Goes back to his script)* Yes, that old hanky of mine. *(He takes it from SUZANNE, kisses it, and returns it to his pocket)* I say, what's that I can hear? *(He looks expectantly towards RICHARD)*
SUZANNE	What's what?

RICHARD is fiddling with the tape deck. He makes a 'keep going' gesture.

| GEORGE | I thought I heard the approach of the 5.38 train, which I was expecting to hear just about now. But perhaps I was just imagining it. *(He starts to improvise)* I'm sure it'll be here any time soon. I mean, there are often delays at this time of year – er, leaves on the line, earthquakes, that sort of thing... |

MAURICE steps in to try and help.

| MAURICE | Er, did I hear you enquiring about the 5.38 train, guvnor? Well, stone the crows me old cock sparra, it's a right palaver and no mistake. Well, I just found out from down the line that it's running late, see. Cos – er, cos – er, cos of its delayed departure from the previous station. *(He peers hopefully at RICHARD who is still struggling with the tape)* Cor, me old plates of meat are playin' up somethin' rotten, today. 'Ere – did I hear you a-sayin' you was a doctor like? You wouldn't fancy a butchers at me old corns while you're a-waitin' like? |
| GEORGE | *(Wrinkling his nose)* Well I'd rather not if it's all the same to you. |

RICHARD waves from the control room and gives a thumbs-up.

MAURICE 'Arf a mo, I do believe I hear it now...

We hear TERRY's voice saying 'Sound effect fifteen', then the sound of ice-cream van chimes.

MAURICE Well, lawks a mercy, and no mistake...

ROSE grabs one of the microphones and blows into it doing a creditable impersonation of a steam train arriving at a station. HERMIONE rummages in the props on the floor and finds a kettle whistle to provide an accompaniment.

MAURICE (*Holding his nose*) Milton Junction – Milton Junction. The train at platform one is the 5.38 for Chelford.

GEORGE Well, I think that's my train – I'd better go. Goodbye Mrs Pargeter. So nice to have met you. Goodbye, Laura old girl. Remember now, be brave. Stiff copper pipes and all that.

HERMIONE Goodbye Alec. Take care.

SUZANNE Goodbye, Doctor. He seems a very nice man, Laura.

HERMIONE Yes, Dulcie. He's... he's... he's going to Africa.

SUZANNE But I thought he was getting the Chelford train.

HERMIONE No Dulcie, next week! Oh, I shall probably never see him again. What am I going to do? How can I ever live without him!

During the following speeches, SUZANNE swivels slightly from side to side as she switches character.

SUZANNE (*As IRIS*) Have you finished with these cups?

SUZANNE (*As DULCIE*) Yes thanks, I think so. What about you, Laura?

SUZANNE (*As IRIS*) I hope you don't think I'm trying to 'urry you, like.

SUZANNE (*As DULCIE*) No, not at all.

SUZANNE (*Wrongly, as DULCIE*) Only, we're closing soon, dearie. And we have to clean up, see.

HERMIONE shakes a finger at SUZANNE.

SUZANNE   What? Oh, I see, sorry. *(As IRIS)* Only, we're closing soon, dearie. And we have to clean up, see.

HERMIONE   No, that's quite all right, we were just going. Oh Dulcie, I feel such a silly. You are such a good friend to me.

SUZANNE   Come along, Laura. Some fresh air's what you need. You'll soon feel better once we're outside.

Enter a cleaner with a large noisy vacuum cleaner. Eventually, after much gesticulating from GEORGE, she is persuaded to turn the thing off.

CLEANER   Well, I'm very sorry I'm sure. I mean, 'ow was I to know you was broadcasting? You hain't got your hon-the-hair light lit, has you. I'm not a bloomin' mind-reader, am I? And look at the mess you're making on that floor. Vacuuming and dusting, that's all I've got you down for. 'Ow am I supposed to run the vacuum over that lot eh, answer me that. I could report you all to Mrs Murgatroyd for this, you know, and then where would you be, eh? Bloomin' hactors. I don't know who they think they are...

The CLEANER exits grumbling to herself.

ROSE   *(As Mrs BASSETT, ad-libbing)* Of course, you can't get the staff these days...

RICHARD switches on the ON THE AIR sign and starts jabbing at his watch and his script.

MAURICE   Oh dear, we're for it. We're running out of time. I think he wants us to skip to the end. That's you, Hermione.

HERMIONE   Righto. *(Turns to end of script)* Published by Samuel French Ltd, 26 Southampton Street, London WC2. All rights reserved. Oh, sorry. *(Turns back a couple of pages)* And so, to cut a long story short. Well shortish, anyway. It was the following week. I'd had an absolutely wretched day in town and took the early train home. Thankfully, that awful Dulcie Pargeter wasn't on board.

> I was feeling pretty beastly – life seemed so empty and meaningless without Alec. As I heard the train pull away from the village station...

ROSE repeats her performance blowing into the microphone. As she does so, we hear the taped sound of a real steam-train blend in with her efforts. The others stop and look at her in admiration until she stops and the sounds continue. They then realise that RICHARD has apparently managed to get the tape sorted out.

> As I heard the train pull away from the village station, all the events of the past few months seemed to flash through my mind. That time at the pictures when we saw 'Jane Eyre'... *(She looks expectantly at RICHARD – we hear the taped sounds of automatic gunfire)* And that afternoon on the boating lake... *(The sound of a cuckoo-clock)* and how funny you looked when you fell in the water *(The sound of a large tree being felled. By now, everyone is looking disgusted at RICHARD's efforts to provide suitable sound effects)* Then there was that lovely day you took me to the races...

From a brown-paper bag in the pile of props, ROSE produces a pair of coconut shells, and clops them together. MAURICE starts improvising a horse race commentary and the others gradually join in, egging him on, cheering enthusiastically and waving their scripts.

MAURICE   And as they come up to the final furlong, in the lead is Cavalcade, Cavalcade closely followed by London Pride, then on the rails in third place is Blithe Spirit. Behind the leaders it's a close run between Private Lives, Bitter-Sweet and Hay Fever with Mrs Worthington the back marker. With a half a furlong to go it's Cavalcade, Cavalcade the leader now being pressed by Blithe Spirit, Blithe Spirit moving up from third place. And as they come towards the line, it's neck and neck between Blithe Spirit and Cavalcade. Blithe Spirit and Cavalcade. And at the line it's Blithe Spirit, Blithe Spirit the winner,

>Cavalcade second, London Pride third and Mrs Worthington fourth.

A mixture of cheers and groans from everyone. GEORGE takes a small piece of paper from his pocket and tears it up like a losing betting slip. Eventually they hear RICHARD knocking on the control room window, jabbing at his watch.

MAURICE   ... and with that I return you to the studio.

HERMIONE I walked through the village in a dream, not knowing or caring what would become of me. Oh, Alec – why did you have to leave me? As I turned the corner into our road, it started to rain quite heavily...

ROSE gets the tray with the tea-pot and strainer, and motions MAURICE to get the waste-paper bin. ROSE and pours tea through the strainer noisily into the bin.

>... but I felt so upset that I hardly seemed to notice. Then, finally, as I crunched up the gravel drive to our house...

MAURICE opens the bag of crisps, spreads them on the tray, then crunches them with his feet.

>... and splashed through the fresh puddles...

ROSE pours some tea onto the tray with the crisps. MAURICE continues his treading.

>... I knew exactly what I had to do. I had to find Fred and tell him everything. Dear, reliable, conventional, decent, trustworthy old Fred. I looked in the drawing room but apart from the crackling fire...

MAURICE picks up the crisp-packet and crinkles it into the microphone.

>and the large tank...

MAURICE makes noises of artillery firing.

>... where the goldfish were swimming peacefully around, the room was deserted. As I entered the kitchen, our dog Trixie greeted me with a chorus of welcoming barks...

MAURICE and ROSE simultaneously start doing completely different sets of barking noises.

> Er, and next door's dog Rover also seemed to be there keeping Trixie company. Oh, where could Fred be? Then Trixie, oh yes and Rover as well, followed me into the hall. With my heart racing, I pounded up the stairs to the landing – the thump of my heavy feet resounding through the house.

MAURICE and ROSE continue barking. ROSE points to the wooden cupboard which they all drag over to the centre and place face down. MAURICE jumps on top and starts pounding enthusiastically on its back which then gives way.

> Feeling sick, I burst into the bathroom. And there, I found Fred. Dear ordinary, reliable, conventional, respectable, decent, stiff upper-lipped, boring, tedious, old Fred. In the bath with Dulcie Pargeter, surrounded by pink bath-towels!

ROSE blows bubbles with a straw in the remains of the lemonade. MAURICE is still barking.

HERMIONE   They seemed not to notice my arrival, so engrossed were they in their passionate embraces.

MAURICE does the kissing sound-effect on his hand into one of the microphones. GEORGE, however, takes SUZANNE into his arms in an enthusiastic embrace. MAURICE stops the sound effect but GEORGE and SUZANNE remain entwined – MAURICE and ROSE start growling in their direction and HERMIONE notices what is going on.

HERMIONE   *(Venomously)* Then suddenly, everything became clear. Oh, what a fool I'd been. I felt an overwhelming torrent of pain and anger welling up inside. It was time I took things into my own hands. *(HERMIONE picks up a rolled-up umbrella from the heap on the floor)* I opened my mouth and let out a loud scream.

HERMIONE rams the umbrella into GEORGE's rear. He emits a loud scream. GEORGE is about to retaliate, but SUZANNE pulls him back to the script. GEORGE grabs the metal waste-paper bin and speaks into it, trying to get an echo.

GEORGE (*As FRED*) Oh my God, Laura, it's you. I wasn't expecting you back so soon, old girl. (*He tips the liquid from the waste-bin over her*)

HERMIONE Obviously! Oh Fred, after all these years, and everything I've done for you. How could you do this to me! (*She slaps him across the face*)

GEORGE Ow! That isn't in the script.

HERMIONE (*Aside, sweetly*) Oh, I am sorry George, my mistake. (*Goes back to script*) And with a woman who was supposed to be my friend.

SUZANNE But Laura, I can explain. You see, there I was in town one day, in Shackleton's, browsing around their linen department – Shackleton's always do such lovely towels don't you think, especially that pastel pink. And their towels are so soft and fluffy. When you drape yourself in one after a hot bath and feel its silky texture gently caressing your bare buttocks and thighs...

GEORGE (*As FRED*) Oh yes, bare buttocks, and thighs, and shoulders, and...

SUZANNE Anyway, who should I bump into in the towel department but Fred. Apparently *he*'s very partial to Shackleton's fluffy pink bath-towels, but it seems you always buy those boring white ones from the co-op.

GEORGE (*Getting a little carried away and fondling SUZANNE*) ... thighs, and buttocks, and breasts, and...

HERMIONE (*As LAURA but ad-libbing*) Shut up! I'm sick of you and your stupid chatter and your painted face and your contact lenses. Here's what you can do with your explanations, Dulcie Pargeter! (*HERMIONE twists SUZANNE's ear*)

SUZANNE   (*As herself*) You bitch, that's not in the script either. Oh, George.

SUZANNE starts crying. GEORGE takes her in his arms to comfort her.

HERMIONE   Well, you're welcome to him that's all I can say. If you want me, you'll find me – in Africa! And with that, I stormed back down the stairs...

MAURICE, who is still stuck inside the cupboard, pulls off one of his shoes and bangs them on the intact piece of the cupboard back.

          With the two dogs still at my heels...

MAURICE and ROSE who have been intermittently yapping, intensify their performance.

GEORGE   (*As FRED, ad-libbing*) Well good riddance is all I can say. Stupid old cow! I don't know how I've put up her with for so long.

HERMIONE   I ran out of the front door and down the long drive...

MAURICE extracts himself from the cupboard and treads the tray contents with his stockinged feet.

HERMIONE   And as I ran, the puddles splashed and the gravel flew in all directions...

HERMIONE pushes MAURICE aside, picks up the tray containing the crisps and lemonade mixture, and tips it over GEORGE's head.

HERMIONE   And so I ran, on and on, through the village and down to the railway station. As I stood on the deserted platform, my heart surged with excitement as I contemplated the prospect of my new life stretching out before me. And there, in the distance, came the sound of the approaching 7.05 train...

Everyone turns to look hopefully at RICHARD. He starts the tape deck and we hear the sound of an approaching steam-train with its whistle blowing. He smiles and gives a thumbs-up sign. Everyone visibly relaxes and smiles.

HERMIONE   The 7.05 train to Milton – and to my future with Alec!

The train gets louder and louder then we hear the deafening sound of a train crash. Everyone is stunned. Blackout except for the ON THE AIR sign, which goes out a second or two later.

THE END.

Making Ends Meet

This one-act play takes a peek behind the scenes at the world's most ineffectual dating agency....

CHARACTERS
FIONA PRENDERGAST – forties/fifties, good-hearted, inept
BEVERLY – Fiona's secretary – twenties, dowdy, cheerful
TREVOR HOPKINS – mid-thirties, awkward, insecure
MRS HOPKINS, Trevor's mother – sixties, dotty
JOANNE – thirty-one, attractive, bright, irreverent
GREGORY CHADWICK – fifties, military, smarmy

The staging of this piece needs to be kept very simple with minimal furniture and props – just a table and two chairs should largely suffice, plus a typewriter and phone. Scene changes need to be kept as short and slick as possible to keep the action flowing. If desired, scene changes can be covered by a brief musical extract – some suggestions are given at the appropriate points in the text.

MUSIC – *Getting to Know You* (from 'The King and I')

SCENE 1. *Inner office of the Fiona Buckingham Introduction Agency.*

FIONA	Honesty. Absolute honesty. That's the first rule in this business, Mr Hopkins. Remember that, and we'll soon find you a kindred spirit. Now then, Trevor, isn't it?
TREVOR	That's right. Trevor... Edmund Hillary Sherpa Tenzing... Hopkins
FIONA	Trevor Ed....
TREVOR	You know. Everest?
FIONA	Ah. Yes.
TREVOR	It was my dad's idea. He thought it might help make me, you know...
FIONA	Let's confine ourselves to Trevor, shall we? Keep it simple.
TREVOR	That's what I usually do. Only you did say absolute honesty.
FIONA	Anyway, there isn't really space.
TREVOR	Whatever you think best, Mrs Buckingham.
FIONA	No, Mr... er, Trevor. We went through all that on the phone. There isn't actually anyone called Fiona Buckingham.
TREVOR	But I thought the woman outside called you Fiona.
FIONA	That's right. I am Fiona.
TREVOR	Oh, I see...
FIONA	But not Fiona Buckingham.
TREVOR	...I think.
FIONA	Good.
TREVOR	What, then?
FIONA	Sorry?

TREVOR	Fiona what, then?
FIONA	We do like to restrict ourselves to first names here, Trevor. All part of our policy of complete confidentiality. One can't be too careful. Strictly entrée nous, some of my past clients have been household names. I couldn't possibly mention anyone specifically, of course. But if I were to say to you 'Exceedingly Good Sausages'... I'm sure you'll apprehend my illusion.
TREVOR	Sausages?
FIONA	Things were all very different then, of course...
TREVOR	I just thought – if I ever needed to ask for you.
FIONA	Halcyon days...
TREVOR	Don't suppose it matters really... Fiona.
FIONA	(*She gives him a blank look then puts on a bright smile*) Now then, Trevor, where were we... age?
TREVOR	Thirty-six, last March.
FIONA	(*Making notes*) Early thirties...
TREVOR	Er, isn't that rather stretching things?
FIONA	You're as young as you feel, Trevor, that's the first rule here. What's a year or two amongst friends?

TREVOR opens his mouth as if to speak but the phone rings.

FIONA	Would you excuse me, Trevor? (*She picks up the phone*) Beverly dear, I did say no calls... Oh. Oh, is he? Oh, all right, put him on. (*She covers the mouthpiece*) Sorry Trevor, it seems that someone is desperate for my attentions... Malcolm! This is a pleasant surprise. Are you? I'm sorry to hear that. Who? Oh, Brenda. Well she's very keen to meet you, Malcolm. Carlisle? Yes, charming part of the world. I know it's a long way from Barnstaple. Oh, I see. I don't have your file in front of me Malcolm, but if we agreed fifty miles maximum then I'm sure... What? Petite? Yes, I do know what it means... in, er, broad terms. Well perhaps it's an old photo. Perhaps she's lost weight since... look, Malcolm, I can tell you're

	the tiniest bit upset, but if you'll just leave it with me, I'll... (*Malcolm has hung up*) Oh dear. Must have been cut off.
TREVOR	Problems?
FIONA	Just a slight clerical error out in the office. All the clients we have to deal with – sacks full of mail every day. Er, not that they don't all get my complete personal attention of course. Now then, Trevor – hobbies. Would you rather a) go hot-air ballooning, b) visit the ballet, or c) have a quiet evening at home playing mah-jong?
TREVOR	I didn't know there was going to be a test.
FIONA	No, Trevor. We have to build up a picture of you. Your personal profile. Surely you read the brochure?
TREVOR	Oh, I see. Is it for the computer?
FIONA	Er, yes. That's right – for the, er, computer. And, of course, for passing on to all your specially selected prospective partners. That's where I come in. I can always tell whether two people are going to hit it off. Don't ask me how, but I'm never wrong. Of course, we're always limited by who's with the agency at any particular moment, but given time I'm absolutely confident we'll...
TREVOR	Is there a parachute?
FIONA	I beg your pardon?
TREVOR	A parachute. You know. For the hot-air balloon...

MUSIC – *Up, Up and Away* **(Johnny Mann Singers)**

SCENE 2. *Living room of TREVOR and his MOTHER's house.*

MOTHER	(*Reading*) Trevor is a sociable, outgoing person, although he also enjoys quiet evenings at home playing m-ha... m-ja...
TREVOR	Mah-Jong. It was either that or hot-air ballooning.

MOTHER	You should have put down balloons. I keep saying you should get more fresh air.
TREVOR	Mother, I do not want to go ballooning. You know how heights affect me.
MOTHER	I expect they'll give you a parachute if you ask them.
TREVOR	I am not going hot-air ballooning!
MOTHER	I was only trying to help. (*Reading*) He enjoys the outdoors and travel. (*To Trevor*) Well, that's one thing you don't get from *me*. In my day, folks liked to stay in their own homes. (*Reading*) He also has a tidy, organised mind. All these aspects of his character are brought together in his favourite pastime of cataloguing travel receipts from public-service vehicles.
TREVOR	She said to put it like that. She said it sounded better than collecting bus-tickets.
MOTHER	Well, I expect she knows about these things. She ought to, the money it's costing.
TREVOR	I did say, but you wouldn't listen.
MOTHER	(*Reading*) Trevor is fond of animals excluding insects but including spiders which are not insects.
TREVOR	I made her put that bit in. In case anybody thought I didn't know the difference. It might put people off if they thought I didn't know.
MOTHER	(*Reading*) Trevor is a strong character but can also be gentle when the need arises. He is articulate, but always willing to listen to both sides. He is decisive but ever ready to take good advice. He is easygoing but always prepared to make a stand when the occasion demands. He has a warm and caring nature and a great deal to give to the right person. (*To TREVOR*) Ah, that's nice. She's got you to a T.
TREVOR	I expect she puts all that for everybody.

MOTHER	Never mind. Long as it does the trick. (*Reading*) Age Early thirties... humh. Height six-foot two! Since when did you grow four inches?
TREVOR	She said it was for the best. Apparently, women have this thing about height so you have to think positive, otherwise they won't even look at you. That's her first rule, 'think positive'. And then you have to try and meet them in a situation where you're sitting down, so they don't notice, like in a pub or a tea-shop.
MOTHER	And how are you supposed to get into this tea-shop without standing up?
TREVOR	She didn't mention that bit. Anyway, before they have time to realise it, you've got to overwhelm them with the size of your personality. That's what Fiona says.
MOTHER	Does she indeed. So, what happens now?
TREVOR	Well, Fiona feeds my details into her computer. To match me up with... you know. Then she chooses which ones to send me. She picks each one, personally. It's all very scientific.
MOTHER	And then what?
TREVOR	I'm not sure. I think we just have to wait and see ...

MUSIC – *Walk Tall* **(Val Doonican)**

SCENE 3. *FIONA is lying face down on a table, mostly covered in a towel. JOANNE is massaging her neck and shoulders.*

FIONA	(*Moaning*) Oooh. Errh. Oooh. Aaah.
JOANNE	Just relax. I don't think I've ever seen you this tense.
FIONA	One of those days, I'm afraid, Joanne. In fact, one of those years the way things are going.
JOANNE	I'm sure it can't be that bad.
FIONA	You just would not believe what I have to endure to earn an honest crust.

JOANNE	I wish *I* could charge what you do. What is it – £950 for five introductions?
FIONA	I do wish you wouldn't make me sound quite so mercenary, Joanne.
JOANNE	I worked it out once – it's nearly two hundred pounds a phone number.
FIONA	And I do have my overheads. Beverly, for instance. I know I don't pay her a lot, but...
JOANNE	That's nearly twenty pounds a digit.
FIONA	It would still be a bargain at twice the price for some of them. I mean, take this afternoon. I've got this little form. Thirty questions – forty-five minutes. That's how it usually goes. An hour at the outside.
JOANNE	Was it that bad?
FIONA	Three hours and seventeen minutes. We spent nearly twenty minutes on one question – 'Do you like animals?'
JOANNE	How could you possibly...?
FIONA	Usually, it's a simple choice between 'yes', 'no' and 'no strong feelings.' But if your name's Trevor Edmund Hillary Sherpa Tenzing Hopkins, apparently you need to have a long debate. About whether it means 'all animals', and in that case whether it includes insects. And if it does include insects, then are we also counting spiders which aren't true insects but which most people treat like insects. Or, on the other hand, if the question is about domestic and farmyard animals...
JOANNE	I get the picture.
FIONA	He would go on about spiders, and you know how I feel about them... ugh!
JOANNE	Easy now. Is his name really...?
FIONA	Apparently, his father had this crack-brained theory it would somehow...
JOANNE	Make him go up in the world?

FIONA	I know I shouldn't complain – he's the first new member in six weeks. We'll soon be down to single figures at this rate. And there are limits to who I can pair people up with. Malcolm in Barnstaple's been through *all* the women except old Doris in Basingstoke.
JOANNE	Some men go for the more mature woman.
FIONA	She's old enough to be his grandmother! And I don't know what I'm going to do with Trevor. I can't afford to lose any more clients. And living over the office doesn't help. If the business goes under, I could be out on the streets. Oh well, that's quite enough of my troubles. How are things going with you, Joanne?
JOANNE	Oh, not so bad. In fact *I* had an awkward customer the other day. Montgomery Bartlett, he called himself. IT consultant or something technical, or so he said. A right tosser. I could tell from the minute he walked in what he was really angling for. Then he started making all these suggestions. You know, extra services – all that sort of thing.
FIONA	Was he upset when you put him straight?
JOANNE	He was more upset by the massage. I really let him have it. The full works. All with a straight face, of course. I bet he ached all over the next day.
FIONA	It must have been quite a performance.
JOANNE	Well, I did once pass the auditions for drama school. That's always been my real ambition – acting.
FIONA	Really, Joanne? I'd never realised.
JOANNE	Yes. Couldn't get a grant, though. You wouldn't believe how much the fees are. But I still dream...
FIONA	I'm sure there's still time.
JOANNE	I don't know about that. Keep those shoulders nice and relaxed. Thirty-two next birthday, me.
FIONA	Forty's the worst. After that you stop counting.
JOANNE	That's better. Well, thirty was bad enough for me.

FIONA   (*Sitting up*) You know, Joanne, I've been thinking. We might just be able to do each other a little favour.

JOANNE   What, you mean find me some more customers?

FIONA   Not exactly. I was thinking more of your acting ambitions.

MUSIC – *Act Naturally* **(The Beatles)**

SCENE 4. *Outer office of the FBIA. BEVERLY is typing slowly and erratically on a manual typewriter. FIONA enters.*

FIONA   Morning, Beverly. Anything in the post?

BEVERLY   Just the usual – gas bill, reminder from the printers, final demand from BT, and Malcolm in Barnstaple is asking for his money back. Oh, and a postcard from the window cleaner – the Maldives. Apparently, the scuba-diving's not been so good this year.

FIONA   Spare me the gory details, dear. I always knew we were in the wrong business. I should get out while you can. You're not a bad-looking girl – I'm sure you could do all sorts of things. Marketing... advertising... window-cleaner's moll. What about these Tupperware parties you're always organising?

BEVERLY   You don't mean...

FIONA   What?

BEVERLY   You're not giving me my notice?

FIONA   Good Lord, no.

BEVERLY   Only I thought... well... with how things have been lately. Every place I've ever worked has given me notice. Or closed down. Or gone bankrupt. My typing *is* getting better. You said so yourself.

FIONA   The sands of destiny have a bit further to turn before I need to let you go, Beverly. And yes, that was a most charming envelope you typed yesterday. I harbour great

	hopes of it reaching its destination. However, nil desperado – once Mr Hopkins' cheque has cleared, the land will again be flowing with fresh-ground coffee and almond croissants. Speaking of which, could you pop the kettle on when you get a chance.
BEVERLY	What would you like me to do with Mr Hopkins?
FIONA	The words 'long walk' and 'short pier' spring to mind. Well, unless any affectionados of the omnibus have suddenly appeared on the files, I suppose we should try and keep him happy for while. There's a new member called Joanne.
BEVERLY	Joanne?
FIONA	Yes. She, er, came in yesterday afternoon. After you'd gone. I, er, typed up her profile myself – it's in the file. I'm sure she'll be just right for Trevor.
BEVERLY	Rightio. Oh, I couldn't find Trevor's photo in his file.
FIONA	The one he brought had him in this most peculiar outfit. He was grinning out from under a ridiculous peaked hat that was far too big for him. Completely unsuitable. I told him it was the wrong size.
BEVERLY	What, the hat?
FIONA	No, the photo. He said he's got another one that might be better.
BEVERLY	A photo?
FIONA	No, a hat. Anyway, he's going to drop it in sometime.
BEVERLY	I'll put down 'awaiting photo' for the time being then, shall I? Oh, I nearly forgot. There was another new enquiry. Some brigadier chap. I put the letter on your desk.
FIONA	A brigadier? And you've been keeping me here chattering all this time. You know, Beverly, I suddenly feel quite extravagant. Run down to the shops and some get some Viennese whirls. I think we may need them...

MUSIC – *Love Letters* **(Ketty Lester)**

SCENE 5. *TREVOR and MOTHER are having breakfast. He is reading a letter.*

MOTHER	Well, what's it say?
TREVOR	Mother! It did say 'Private' on the front in case you hadn't noticed.
MOTHER	Well then?
TREVOR	It's a woman.
MOTHER	And...?
TREVOR	And what?
MOTHER	Ooh, give it here. (*Reading*) Joanne... hmhm! Joanne is petite, with blonde hair and brown eyes, and is in her mid-twenties. She is a sociable, outgoing person although she also enjoys quiet evenings at home playing...
TREVOR	Mah-jong
MOTHER	I can read, Trevor, thank you very much. ... playing mah-jong. Working as a caring professional, Joanne is a strong character but can also be gentle when the need arises. She is articulate, but always willing to listen to both sides. She is decisive but ever ready to take good advice. She is easygoing but always prepared to make a stand when the occasion demands. She has a warm and caring nature and a great deal to give to the right person.
TREVOR	I suppose she sounds all right.
MOTHER	She sounds very nice. I think you might have a lot in common...
TREVOR	There's no mention of public-service vehicles.
MOTHER	In fact, it could even be you they were describing.
TREVOR	Or spiders.
MOTHER	Perhaps they didn't have anyone else in the computer who put down buses.

TREVOR   You'd have thought there might have been one or two, in all those hundreds of people.

MOTHER   Perhaps they weren't the right age. Or too far away. She put down mja-what-ever-it-is – you'll have that to talk about. At least she didn't put down balloons. Then where would you have been? Don't let your porridge go cold, son.

TREVOR   Mother, I've never even played mah-jong. I wouldn't know a mah-jong set if it fell off a luggage rack and hit me on the head. (*He pushes the dish away*). I'm not hungry.

MOTHER   I was only trying to look on the bright side. I did think you'd try and make the effort after all the money it's costing. This is all for your benefit you know, Trevor.

TREVOR   Yes, mother.

MOTHER   So what happens now, then?

TREVOR   Well, first, the agency send me *her* details. Which is what they've just done. Then if I want to meet her, I have to contact the agency to tell them to send her my details. Then if she likes the sound of me, she gets back in touch with the agency to say it's all right and then they send me her phone number.

MOTHER   If we're not all dead in our graves by then. Couldn't they just give you an album to look through. Pick out the ones you like the look of. I could come and help you.

MOTHER   You can't rush these things, Mother. That's their rule number one, so Fiona says. Anyway, then I phone her up...

MOTHER   Who?

TREVOR   This Joanne. Assuming she wants to. She probably won't.

MOTHER   Course she will.

TREVOR   And then we... you know.

MOTHER   You declare your intentions.

TREVOR	Something like that. I don't know. Fiona was a bit vague about what happens then.
MOTHER	Invite her round for tea. That'd be nice.
TREVOR	Yes, mother.
MOTHER	You could make her one of those cakes you used to do for me. Victoria Sponge. You haven't done one of them for a long time.

MUSIC – *Tea for Two* **(Tommy Dorsey)**

SCENE 6. *Fiona's Inner Office*

FIONA	Honesty. Absolute honesty. That's the first rule in this business, Mr Chadwick.
CHADWICK	Actually, it's *Brigadier* Chadwick, if you want to be strict about it. But that was all a good many years ago now, of course.
FIONA	Well, we don't like to be too formal. Er, Gregory, isn't it?
CHADWICK	Indeed, dear lady. Gregory. From the Greek, as I'm sure you know, meaning 'to be watchful'.
FIONA	Of course. How fascinating. Do help yourself to a Viennese whirl.
CHADWICK	Delightful. The simple pleasures of domesticity. Of which I have been sadly deprived since my unhappy loss.
FIONA	Your late wife?
CHADWICK	Indeed. A perfect bloom whose fragrance will forever linger in the memory – as I was only observing to the head gardener this very morning.
FIONA	You must have been very close.
CHADWICK	We were. But it's almost a year now and, well, life at the Manor House must go on.
FIONA	Courage, Gregory. Courage. The *head* gardener you said.

CHADWICK	Fred Glossop. Been with the family donkey's years.
FIONA	So there's more than one gardener then, over at the... Manor House.
CHADWICK	Naturally. Couldn't possibly manage an estate that size with just the one.
FIONA	Indeed not. Er, how big did you say the estate was?
CHADWICK	Oh, seven or eight...
FIONA	Acres?
CHADWICK	Thousand acres. Look, I'm pretty hopeless at all this kind of business, you know. Cynthia – my wife – was the first, the only woman I ever...
FIONA	I understand.
CHADWICK	(*Getting a little emotional*) In fact, it was she who proposed, you know. On the yacht. Cowes week, back in '75.
FIONA	There, there.
CHADWICK	I don't know what she'd think of all this. Perhaps I shouldn't have come. Perhaps I should go.
FIONA	(*Sharply*) No! (*Recovering*) I mean, no I'm sure she'd say you were doing the right thing.
CHADWICK	Perhaps you're right. Better see it through now I've come this far. I believe there's some sort of questionnaire (*he pronounces it 'kestionnaire'*).
FIONA	A few tiny details – er, just for the computer.
CHADWICK	Well then, fire away.
FIONA	Right. Number one – hobbies. Would you rather a) go hot-air ballooning, b) visit the ballet, or c) have a quiet evening at home playing mah-jong...
CHADWICK	Hmm, that's rather a sticky one. Er, am I allowed to ask – I've always wondered about these balloon chappies – does one get a parachute?

MUSIC – *Come Fly with Me* **(Frank Sinatra)**

SCENE 7. *TREVOR is calling JOANNE from a phone-box.*

TREVOR	Hello. Is that Joanne?
JOANNE	Yes?
TREVOR	This is Trevor Hop... oh no, I'm not supposed to say that am I?
JOANNE	Trevor?
TREVOR	From the agency. I got your details.
JOANNE	Oh, right.
TREVOR	Yes. So I'm, er, phoning you up.
JOANNE	Yes?
TREVOR	To, er... To, er, well – you know.
JOANNE	(*Teasing*) Try and sell me some double-glazing?
TREVOR	No! To, er... oh dear. To, er, say hello...
JOANNE	Yes, you've already done that.
TREVOR	Have I? Oh, yes. And to, er...
JOANNE	Invite me out?
TREVOR	What? Oh, right, yes. That's it
JOANNE	Inviting me out already! Fast worker, aren't you? I can see I'm going to have to watch my step with you. I do like a man who knows what he wants and goes out and gets it. It said you were decisive.
TREVOR	Did it?
JOANNE	So, you old smooth talker, you – where were you planning on taking me?
TREVOR	I don't know. I hadn't got that far. I hadn't even got this far.
JOANNE	We could drive out in the country and find somewhere.
TREVOR	Find somewhere? For what?
JOANNE	For a meal, of course. There's Alberto's out on the Woodstock Road. Or the Chateau Blanc over at Great Marston is always very nice. Do you like French cuisine?

TREVOR	They have quiche in the canteen at work sometimes. Mother won't eat foreign food – it upsets her. I quite often get us fish and chips. Actually, I think *they're* from Madeira.
JOANNE	What are?
TREVOR	The people who run the fish and chip shop. Only I haven't told mother. I thought it was probably best.
JOANNE	Well, there's always Italian, or Thai... when do you want to pick me up?
TREVOR	Pick you up?
JOANNE	You do have a car?
TREVOR	Oh. Ah. Er... it's... at the garage. Being repaired. Big job, I'm afraid. The, er, manifold outlet sprocket. I'll probably have to come on the bus.
JOANNE	The bus!
TREVOR	Hang on, the pips are going. (*He inserts more coins*) Hello. Are you still there?
JOANNE	Yes, I'm still here.
TREVOR	We do have a phone but mother doesn't go out much so it's a bit... (*Pause*) Whereabouts do you live?
JOANNE	Near the cemetery. Macintyre Road.
TREVOR	That's easy. The number 12, every twenty minutes – 03, 23 and 43 past the hour from Comer Gardens. Is Thursday all right?
JOANNE	Yes, I think so.
TREVOR	I'll get the 7.43. You can get on at the end of Macintyre Road – should be there at about 7.56. I'll be inside.
JOANNE	Well, I didn't think you'd be on the roof.
TREVOR	No, I meant downstairs.
JOANNE	Oh, I see.
TREVOR	Sitting down.
JOANNE	Sitting down? No, I won't ask. So, how will I recognise you? There wasn't a photo in with your details.

TREVOR	What do people usually do?
JOANNE	Anything. Red carnation in the button hole. Rolled up copy of the Times?
TREVOR	I've got a hat I could wear. With a peak on the front. You know – like a bus conductor's...

MUSIC – *Some Enchanted Evening* **(from 'South Pacific')**

SCENE 8. *Fiona's Inner Office*

FIONA	(*Writing*) Gregory has a warm and caring nature and – how about – a great deal to give to the right person.
CHADWICK	I couldn't have put it better myself.
FIONA	You're a very special person, Gregory. I could tell it from the very first second you walked through that door.
CHADWICK	You're too kind.
FIONA	Well, I should know. You wouldn't believe some of the men we get in here. Personality! You'd get better conversation out of a garden gnome. And as for personal hygiene, well...
CHADWICK	Really?
FIONA	I've had to open the windows on more than occasion. I sometimes wonder how I... you don't mind my confiding in you like this, do you?
CHADWICK	Er, no, er...
FIONA	It's just that, since the loss of my own dear, departed husband...
CHADWICK	I *am* sorry. As you still employ the title of 'Mrs', I naturally assumed...
FIONA	A small gesture to his memory. As I was saying – once in a while, like this afternoon for example, someone comes along who seems to make it all worthwhile. Someone in whom one feels able to... (*Chadwick looks at his watch*) Is anything wrong?

CHADWICK	Oh, no, no. It's just that I told Hemmings – the chauffeur – to meet me at four. Must get back.
FIONA	Ah, the demands of a large estate. Now, we haven't talked about the little matter of our, er, fee. Did Beverly...?
CHADWICK	Oh, yes indeed. I've got the cheque just here in my... Oh dear, silly me.
FIONA	What is it, Gregory?
CHADWICK	I've just realised. I put the cheque into the pocket of my other jacket. I've come out without my wallet, cheque-book or anything.
FIONA	Not to worry. Any time. Pop it in the post if you like.
CHADWICK	Of course. You've been so very kind. I was wondering... Fiona...
FIONA	Yes, Gregory?
CHADWICK	Look, you must say if I'm speaking out of turn. But you've been so helpful... would you do me the honour of letting me take you out to dinner. You know, as a sort of dry run. Purely on a business footing, of course. Well? What do you say?

MUSIC – *I'm Just a Girl Who Can't Say No* **(from 'Oklahoma')**

SCENE 9. *Outer office of the FBIA. BEVERLY is typing in her usual manner. FIONA enters, full of the joys of spring, carrying a bunch of carnations.*

FIONA	Good morning, Beverly. Isn't it a beautiful day? I've just been walking through the park. It really is delightful at this time of year. Could you find a vase for these when you've a minute.
BEVERLY	He'll catch you one of these days.
FIONA	Who will?
BEVERLY	The park keeper – taking his flowers.

FIONA	Yes, Beverly.
BEVERLY	So... present from an admirer, then?
FIONA	Can't I treat myself to a bunch of carnations without a three-hour inquisition?
BEVERLY	Actually, you just missed him?
FIONA	Who?
BEVERLY	Who do you think? The brigadier.
FIONA	Gregory? He was here?
BEVERLY	On the phone, about this evening. Apparently, his chauffeur's broken his arm, so could he meet you there at seven-thirty. He's booked you a taxi. He said if he didn't hear from you, he'd assume it was all right.
FIONA	Perhaps I'd better ring him anyway.
BEVERLY	He said he'd be tied up all day. With his stock-broker or something. But you can leave a message on his machine.
FIONA	You two *were* having a nice cosy little chat by the sound of it. I hope you're not getting any ideas.
BEVERLY	You must be joking. He's a bit ancient. I couldn't see *him* down at my aerobics class. Tea dance at the town hall'd be more his scene. A grand ball at his mansion, now I could probably go for that. Anyway, he seemed more interested our computer system than in me.
FIONA	Computer system!
BEVERLY	Don't worry. I said I left all that side of things to you. Now, shall I get some water for these flowers?
FIONA	On second thoughts Beverly, I'll take them upstairs to the flat. I'd better get started on making myself look presentable for this evening. (*BEVERLY looks at her watch*) Yes, I know it's only ten o'clock but it's a long job. You can give me shout if you need me.
BEVERLY	There was one other thing. Brenda – you know, in Carlisle?
FIONA	Why do I have a feeling I'm not going to like this?

BEVERLY	Well, she's sent in a complaint. About Malcolm. The one in Barnstaple.
FIONA	But she's never even met him.
BEVERLY	She says it shouldn't count as an introduction because they only spoke for five minutes on the phone and he wouldn't go up there because he said it was too far. *And he was her asking personal questions about her figure.* So she says.
FIONA	What does she expect us to do? Drug him and deposit him trussed up in a mail bag on Carlisle station. All right, send her a 'Dear Esteemed'.
BEVERLY	Dear esteemed and valued client, Due to a computer fault beyond our control...
FIONA	That's the one. Now, Beverly, Tempus Fujitsu. If anyone asks, I shall be in conference with a large jar of carrot and cucumber cream for the rest of the morning.

MUSIC – *The Trolley Song* **(from 'Meet Me in St Louis')**

SCENE 10. *Upper deck of a bus.*

JOANNE	Oh, here you are. I was looking for you downstairs.
TREVOR	It was full up so I had to come up here. I did wave but the windows are all a bit steamed up.
JOANNE	There was a chap downstairs wearing a cap. I didn't *think* it was you. He was with this woman – she was starting to give me funny looks. (*Pause*) I haven't been on a bus for ages.
TREVOR	I use them all the time. Er, when the car's being repaired that is.
JOANNE	How's the exhaust sprocket or whatever it was?
TREVOR	They're having trouble getting the parts. Could take months, they reckon.

JOANNE   I'd forgotten the view you get from up here. Look, you can see right inside that bedroom window. What *is* he doing? You could probably catch people at all sorts if you went past often enough. They must know people can see them. Perhaps they're all exhibitionists, you know – leave the curtains open on purpose. Are you all right? You look a bit pale.

TREVOR   I usually sit downstairs. It's not so high up.

JOANNE   I can't argue with that.

TREVOR   Fifteen foot ten inches.

JOANNE   I beg your pardon?

TREVOR   The height of this bus. Fifteen foot ten inches.

JOANNE   You don't say.

TREVOR   4.82 metres if you prefer metric. I usually work in feet and inches myself.

JOANNE   (*Pause*) That's a nice suit. Is it new?

TREVOR   Mother said I ought to wear it. Smarten myself up a bit. It's my interview suit. You know, for interviews.

JOANNE   Oh, really?

TREVOR   And funerals. This feels a bit like an interview.

JOANNE   Well, so long as it doesn't feel like a... You just need to try and relax a bit. (*Pause*) We can talk about anything you like. TV. Music. Holidays. Buses, even. Well, maybe not buses. It's not one of my strong subjects.

TREVOR   (*Pause*) So, how do *you* get to work, then? Your form said you do some kind of social work.

JOANNE   (*Snorts*) That's one way of putting it.

TREVOR   What, battered children and things?

JOANNE   (*Sardonically*) More like deprived old men sometimes.

TREVOR   It must give you a really warm glow inside.

JOANNE   Are you trying to be funny?

TREVOR   No. Honest. I was just... Look, the thing is... well, the thing is... this is the first time I've done this.

JOANNE	What – with Fiona, you mean?
TREVOR	No...
JOANNE	Oh, right. First time with an introduction agency? It's nothing to be ashamed of. Lots of people do it these days.
TREVOR	That's not what I meant.
JOANNE	Then what... I can't be the first girl you've taken out on the town. Trevor? Oh, God. That is what you mean.
TREVOR	I'm sorry. It was all my mother's idea. I know she's right, but... look, I'm thirty-six, I'm five-foot seven, I don't have a car, I've never had a girl-friend, and I can't play mah-jong! (*The bell pings*) Joanne! Where are you going? Joanne! Come back!

MUSIC – *Ticket to Ride* **(The Beatles)**

SCENE 11. *The Chateau Blanc Restaurant*

CHADWICK	Now, my dear – more champagne?
FIONA	Gregory, this is perfectly delightful. I've always wanted to come to the Chateau Blanc. I wish you'd warned me though. I feel positively underdressed.
CHADWICK	Nonsense, Fiona, you look very elegant. In fact I'd go so far as to say you were the most beautiful woman in the room.
FIONA	Now Gregory, you shouldn't tease.
CHADWICK	I meant every single word. Now, what shall we drink to?
FIONA	Something to celebrate your search for Mrs Right. I know – Happy Hunting!
CHADWICK	The very thing. Happy Hunting! (*They chink glasses*) Now, tell me about this fascinating business of yours. I find it all totally intriguing.
FIONA	Oh, there's not much to tell. I always say it's like being a cordon bleu chef. Blending together the right ingredients

	to create the perfect dish – carrot and coriander, broccoli and stilton...
CHADWICK	Prunes and custard? Sorry. Old favourite of mine from the officers' mess.
FIONA	I can't really explain it – I suppose you could say it's a gift.
CHADWICK	It must be very satisfying.
FIONA	Lots of paperwork, of course, but then Beverly's a great help.
CHADWICK	Ah yes, Beverly – your factotum.
FIONA	Well, she's never going to win any prizes for her typing, but she does know how to handle the clients. In case they have any little difficulties.
CHADWICK	Difficulties?
FIONA	It can be a very emotional time, Gregory, as a man of your sensitivity will appreciate. If Miss A sets her heart on meeting Mr B, but Mr B doesn't reciprocate... I'm sure you can understand. A shoulder to cry on, that's what we're there for. Beverly can be a real diplomat on occasions.
CHADWICK	I don't know how you manage to cope with it all. Though you do have the computer of course.
FIONA	Computer?
CHADWICK	To sift through all those thousands of clients on your database. I was perusing your brochure earlier on.
FIONA	Oh, *that* computer. Yes, it's a great boon. We couldn't possibly manage without it.
CHADWICK	What have you got – PC or Macintosh? Sorry, bit of a hobby of mine, computers. I'm a Mac man, myself, I'm afraid.
FIONA	Really? I'd never have guessed. I'm afraid Beverly looks after all that side of things. I just look at the, er, out-prints. Casting my chef's eye over things.

CHADWICK	Of course. Only I was wondering where you had it tucked away.
FIONA	Tucked away?
CHADWICK	The old number-cruncher. I couldn't spot the VDU in your office. My Mac Pro takes up half a desk. And that's not including the printer.
FIONA	Is that so? Exactly the same problem with us – far too much space. So we keep it, er, in a cupboard. Locked away. Out of sight.
CHADWICK	Safe and secure from prying eyes.
FIONA	Exactly.
CHADWICK	The ventilation must be a problem.
FIONA	Ventilation?
CHADWICK	For the machine. I mean, you know how hot CPUs run on some systems.
FIONA	Well, I think Beverly gives it an airing now and again. Oh, look – here's the waiter. I'm starving. You know Gregory, I think I may have the oysters after all.

MUSIC – *Food, Glorious Food* **(from 'Oliver')**

SCENE 12. *The Happy Haddock Fish Bar*

TREVOR	Salt and vinegar?
JOANNE	Oh, go on then. Let's splash out. Trevor!
TREVOR	Sorry. You can use my serviette if you like.
FIONA	I've never been in here before. The Happy Haddock, is that what it's called? They seem to know you though.
TREVOR	I often come in here if I've been out on a spot.
JOANNE	A spot?
TREVOR	You know, new vehicles, or a new design of ticket. Did you know that in the past seven months, Midland Red have tried out four different types of ticket roll. Trouble

	with the ink binding to the paper. Keeps coming off on people's hands. I have heard rumours that they're thinking of trying a new type of ribbon from Germany. Oh, they know about tickets do the Germans.
JOANNE	The view from this window's very, er, handy.
TREVOR	You get all the out-of-town buses coming out this end. Not many this time of day though.
JOANNE	I suppose not. Specially on a weekday evening... until the summer timetable starts, of course.
TREVOR	Are you taking the mickey?
JOANNE	No! All right, maybe just a little bit.
TREVOR	I thought you'd made a bolt for it. When you shot off down the stairs like that.
JOANNE	Well, unless you were planning to entertain me down by the cattle market, I thought we'd better get off quick.
TREVOR	Sorry. I hadn't been looking.
JOANNE	Distracted by my alluring charms. That's what you're supposed to say. Didn't anyone ever tell you?
TREVOR	I don't remember. I don't think so. (*Pause*) Did you ever go round the cattle market – when you were little? My mother always used to take me during the school holidays. Wednesday mornings.
JOANNE	I remember going once.
TREVOR	They were always big and steaming. The cows.
JOANNE	The smell was horrible. Mess all over the floor.
TREVOR	All mooing away like mad. Almost as if they knew...
JOANNE	The lambs were all right, I suppose. Their little black faces.
TREVOR	Mooo...
JOANNE	Baaa...
TREVOR	Mooooooo...
JOANNE	Baaaa... Baaaa...
TREVOR	That woman thinks we're barmy.

JOANNE	Oh dear... I feel a bit sheepish. (*Collapses into giggles*)
TREVOR	She can think what she likes... I won't kowtow to anybody. (*Joanne starts laughing uncontrollably*) Moooooo...
JOANNE	Hello Mr Cow... fleece to meet you.
TREVOR	Did you hear about the bomb that landed in a field and then got eaten by a bull? It was abominable. (*Both now laughing hysterically*)
JOANNE	Oh that's awful.
TREVOR	I know. I'm in a really daft mood.... moood... mooooood!

MUSIC – *Happy Talk* **(from 'South Pacific')**

SCENE 13. *The Chateau Blanc Restaurant*

CHADWICK	So there we were, head keeper and myself, two o'clock in the morning, and would you believe it, this damned fellow actually did have a receipt in his pocket for four pheasants. From some butcher's shop over in Upton.
FIONA	So you had to let him go?
CHADWICK	Well, he was on a public footpath, so what else could we do? Only then, a few days later, we discovered that this butcher's shop had closed down six months before. Must have got hold of some of their old stationery, I suppose.
FIONA	The effrontery of some people.
CHADWICK	Not like the old days eh? Everything done on a handshake. Not that a young thing like you would remember what *I* call the old days.
FIONA	Gregory, you're so sweet.
CHADWICK	If I am, it's all because of your company, my dear. Well, I suppose we'd better be wending our way. Let's have a look at the damage.
FIONA	You must let me pay my share.
CHADWICK	Nonsense. I invited you, remember.

FIONA	Well, if you insist.
CHADWICK	Now, then. I'm sure I had the old cheque book in here somewhere. No. No. Oh blast. I know what's happened. I changed my jacket at the last minute. Look, this is frightfully embarrassing I seem to have come out without a bean. Looks like I'll have to stay all night and do the washing up for them.
FIONA	Don't be silly Gregory. Let me get it. We can, er, sort it out later. Pass me over the bill.
CHADWICK	This is awfully decent of you, Fiona. Fiona? You've gone a bit pale, old girl.
FIONA	No, I'm all right. It's just a little more than I was expecting.
CHADWICK	And all worth every penny, my dear. It *was* rather a good champagne. Look, I'll drop by and square things up with you first thing in the morning.
FIONA	Gregory, there are far more important things in life than money – that's always been my first rule. Now can I tempt you back for a nightcap?
CHADWICK	How could I refuse such an enticing proposal? You see, Fiona, I'd like to get to know you better. Much, much better...

MUSIC – *Tonight* **(from 'West Side Story')**

SCENE 14. *City Street. Night*

TREVOR	Are you warm enough?
JOANNE	Fine. I just needed to walk off that fish and chips.
TREVOR	Didn't you like it?
JOANNE	It was very nice. A bit filling. And the knickerbocker glory was probably a mistake. I'd almost forgotten they existed. You know, like when you sometimes see old adverts for things they don't make any more. Like

	Wonderloaf and Cherry-B. And those old washing powders – Omo and Oxydol.
TREVOR	I didn't think you'd be old enough to remember all those. Your form said mid-twenties.
JOANNE	Yours said early thirties.
TREVOR	That was Fiona's idea. Anyway, she said age wasn't important – between friends.
JOANNE	I think she's probably right.
TREVOR	Have you been with the agency long? I mean, you're really… I wouldn't have thought you'd have much trouble, you know… finding someone.
JOANNE	No – I'm, er, pretty new to all this myself. Anyway, tell me some more about you. Where is it you work?
TREVOR	The Council Offices. You know, down at the end of Broad Street.
JOANNE	Oh, really? What is it you do exactly?
TREVOR	Nothing very exciting. General Services. Making sure street lamps get repaired. Or that people look after their allotments properly. Approving the names for new roads. All that kind of thing.
JOANNE	It sounds really interesting. So you mean, if I was a builder and I wanted to call a street on my new estate Barry Manilow Boulevard, you'd decide whether to allow it or not.
TREVOR	There's lots of things to consider. Whether it might be confused with any similar name in the area – say there was a Hairy Mandible Boulevard a few miles away.
JOANNE	Or if it was a really long name. Hans Christian Andersen Crescent. Or one of those stupid people who get called after all the players in a football team.
TREVOR	Has Fiona been saying something?
JOANNE	What about?

TREVOR	It doesn't matter. Anyway, it's the parents who pick the names. You can't blame the person who has to walk round with them for the rest of their life.
JOANNE	I wasn't saying you should.
TREVOR	Right.
JOANNE	OK. (*Pause*) Can I ask you something? You *were* joking about me being the first girl you've ever taken out.
TREVOR	No. Well, sort of. It's been ages. Years and years. You might as well be the first.
JOANNE	Did something happen? If you don't mind me asking.
TREVOR	It was after my dad died. Mother went all to pieces. Wouldn't go out of the house, not even the garden. I had to do all the shopping and the cooking and stuff.
JOANNE	Wasn't there anyone to help – social services or something?
TREVOR	We had home helps for a bit, but mother always used to fall out with them. Accuse them of stealing. Or moving things so she couldn't find them. All sorts. In the end, it was simplest for me to do everything.
JOANNE	And is she still...
TREVOR	She's a lot better now, but... well, she is getting on bit. Then, suddenly, after years of moaning every time I went out, she starts saying I ought to get myself someone. And as it didn't look like I could manage it on my own... The money's from some insurance policy.
JOANNE	So what's made her...
TREVOR	I don't know. Perhaps she thinks it'd be better with another woman about. To help look after her. It gets a bit embarrassing at times, you know, for a man. She'd rather be dead than go into a home.
JOANNE	Oh, Trevor...
TREVOR	She said we had to do this properly. It's how my dad would have wanted things done. If a thing's worth doing... that's what he used to say.

JOANNE	What was your father? You know, what did he do?
TREVOR	Worked on the buses. Conductor. Thirty-three years. Took early retirement when they went one-man operated.
JOANNE	Was that his? That hat of yours. Was it his conductor's hat?
TREVOR	They don't normally let you keep them. Property of the rate-payers. But they let him keep his.
JOANNE	Trevor – this agency of Fiona's. It may not be such a good idea, you know.
TREVOR	What do you mean? I've already met you, haven't I? I'm sure mother will like you.
JOANNE	Look, Trevor. I shouldn't start building your hopes up too high.
TREVOR	What do you mean? I can see you again, can't I? Joanne?

MUSIC – *I Could Be Happy With You* **(from 'The Boyfriend')**

SCENE 15. *Suburban street. Night.*

FIONA	(*To Taxi-driver, off*) That's all right. Keep the change.
CHADWICK	Look, this is awfully decent of you, Fiona. I can't apologise enough.
FIONA	Nonsense, Gregory – what are friends for?
CHADWICK	Today of all days for my chauffeur to break his leg. Anyway, I've got to be in town first thing tomorrow, so I've got a room booked at the George Hotel. I can easily walk it from here.
FIONA	You're not escaping that easily. I did promise you a nightcap, remember. It's the least I can do after such a wonderful evening.
CHADWICK	Fiona. I can't say how much I've enjoyed it too. You've been like the warm savannah breeze sweeping away my dusty old cobwebs,

FIONA	You do say such nice things. By the way Gregory, your chauffeur – how is his, er, leg?
CHADWICK	He'll be out of action for a while, I'm afraid. Awful nuisance, but can't be helped.
FIONA	Here we are. Just round at the side there. (*They enter the hallway and switch on lights*) Straight up the stairs.
CHADWICK	Actually, I was meaning to ask you, before we go up. There's a very fine ceramic on your secretary's desk.
FIONA	Is there?
CHADWICK	You must know the one I mean. The tiger perched on the rocks. I noticed it when I was here for my little interview.
FIONA	Oh, that old thing.
CHADWICK	It did remind me of my days in Africa. Roaming the savannah, tracking the big cats for hours on end. And fine art is rather a hobby of mine. Would you mind awfully if I had another look?
FIONA	Be my guest.
CHADWICK	Magnificent creature. All that brooding strength. It does take me back, I must say.
FIONA	I can't say I've ever noticed. It was here when I took over the place. In fact, I almost threw it away.
CHADWICK	Look Fiona, as it's getting on a bit, and we do have your reputation to consider, why don't you nip upstairs to fetch the old drinkie-poos. I'll just slip in and chat to Mr Tiger about the good old days.
FIONA	Er, well, yes. Perhaps you're right. Wouldn't want the neighbours talking. Are you sure you'll be all right?
CHADWICK	Don't you worry about me, I'll just amuse myself down here. Other people's rooms are always so... revealing. Don't you find?

MUSIC – *I Tawt I Taw a Puddy Cat* **(Mel Blanc)**

SCENE 16. *Suburban street. Night.*

TREVOR	Joanne! Can you just stop a minute? Please? Was it something I said? Couldn't you at least just tell me.
JOANNE	It's not you at all Trevor, it's me... No, it's not, it's *her*! It was all her idea.
TREVOR	Who? What idea?
JOANNE	Fiona. Going out with her clients.
TREVOR	But I got your form. It was me who asked you out. We got matched up on the database.
JOANNE	Trevor, there is no database. In fact, there are hardly any clients.
TREVOR	I don't understand. Then why did I get your details?
JOANNE	I'm doing it as a favour for Fiona. We've got this arrangement. You see, sometimes, like at the moment, there aren't many women on the books. I mean, you're really nice, Trevor, but even with Fiona's helping hand, it's probably going to take a while to find you someone...
TREVOR	You mean no woman in her right mind is going to want to go out with me.
JOANNE	No! What I meant was... it all takes time and people sometimes start getting miserable or impatient or wanting their money back. So that's where I come in.
TREVOR	Where do you come in?
JOANNE	Fiona would kill me if she knew I was telling you all this. She's pretending I'm on her books and sending out my details to people. And then – well I'm not bad-looking – so if people say they'd like to meet me, we can go out and have a nice time. I *have* had a good time, tonight, Trevor, really I have. Then people can feel like they're getting somewhere. You know, like there's hope.
TREVOR	But there's not, is there? It's all a big con.
JOANNE	Things have been a bit hard for her. She's just trying to give things a boost. Like the computer. I think she's

	almost convinced herself she has got one. They don't even have a word-processor. But she really is good. She can spot a match in the unlikeliest of people.
TREVOR	And what about that stupid questionnaire? It took hours. Complete waste of time by the sound of it.
JOANNE	She says forms help people open up. Like if you're in a bank or somewhere and they bring out a form. Address? Age? Salary? Before you know it, you've given them your life story. And all you went in for was tell them your new address.
TREVOR	That still doesn't change things. You're not here because you wanted to meet me, but because Fiona's paying you. And I bet that afterwards you'll say you're really sorry but you don't want to see me again.
JOANNE	Something like that.
TREVOR	It makes it all sound like you're a – you know. One of those women. You're not are you? Mother would have a fit if she knew.
JOANNE	It's not like that, Trevor. *I'm* not like that. Honestly. Look, people like you, in your position, they often find it really hard to... oh, I don't know. Look, I'm only telling you all this because...
TREVOR	Because you feel sorry for me?
JOANNE	No! Because you're right. I agree with you. If you wanted an escort for the evening, there's plenty of places you could go. And at half the price you're paying Fiona. You see, I count as one of your five introductions. So the past three hours have cost you the best part of two hundred pounds.
TREVOR	Mother'll go spare. She mustn't find out. She's pinned all her hopes on this.
JOANNE	She doesn't have to find out. I won't tell her.
TREVOR	What am I going to *do*?

JOANNE	I've had enough of all this. If Fiona wants to run an introduction agency – fine. An escort agency – no problem. But she just has to be straight with people. Look, it's not that late and her place is only two minutes walk from here. If she's still up, or even if she isn't, we're going to have it out with her – now!

MUSIC – *Let's Call the Whole Thing Off* **(Fred Astaire)**

SCENE 17. *Fiona's outer office. CHADWICK is rifling through the office contents. FIONA enters with tray of drinks.*

FIONA	Here we are, sorry to have been so... Gregory, what are you doing?
CHADWICK	Oh, Fiona. I didn't hear you. I was, er, just looking for some scrap paper. To, er, make a note of the sculptor's name. It might be worth getting it valued, you know. I've got a little man who could look at it for you.
FIONA	Gregory, I may be a lot of things, but I am not stupid. It is not an undiscovered work of art, it's a nasty cheap plaster ornament. Even Oxfam wouldn't take it. I think you have some explaining to do.
CHADWICK	Steady on, old girl. Haven't got the right glasses on, that's all. I must have...
FIONA	Don't tell me – left them in your other jacket?
CHADWICK	Precisely.
FIONA	So, Gregory – if that's your real name, which I very much doubt – what's this all about? If it's money you're after, you're going to be very disappointed. You've probably got more than I have, and that's not saying a lot if this evening's little performance is anything to go by.
CHADWICK	I'm sorry, dear lady, I'm not sure I...
FIONA	Oh yes? You must think I was born yesterday. This invisible chauffeur of yours with the broken leg. Or was

	it his arm? Or perhaps he just disappeared up his own exhaust pipe.
CHADWICK	I can assure you that Hemmings is...
FIONA	And a very good friend of mine who used to live in Kenya, once told me quite categorically that finding a tiger in Africa is about as likely as meeting a man who isn't egotistical, patronising, scheming and deceitful!
CHADWICK	In that case, my dear Fiona, there's only one thing for it...

CHADWICK moves towards FIONA. She screams and drops the tray.

FIONA	Oh, my God! Gregory! Help!

TREVOR and JOANNE enter.

FIONA	Trevor, help me. Please.
CHADWICK	What the devil...

TREVOR picks something off her sleeve and runs offstage with it.

FIONA	Oh, thank God. Thank God...
TREVOR	(*Coming back in*) It's all right. I've put it outside. You probably just disturbed it.
FIONA	I've never seen a spider that big in my whole life. And this... useless idiot was just standing there like a...
JOANNE	Montgomery Bartlett!
CHADWICK	Joanne?
TREVOR	Mr Chadwick!
CHADWICK	Hopkins!
FIONA	Er, I hate to interrupt on this touching reunion, but do I understand that you both know Brigadier Chadwick?
JOANNE	That's not what he was calling himself last week when I was giving him a massage. He told me he worked in...
TREVOR	He works in the Trading Standards Department at the Council Offices. Up on the first floor.
FIONA	Trading Standards?
CHADWICK	You will, in due course, be receiving a summons regarding a number of offences under the Trade

	Descriptions and Consumer Protection Acts. Not to mention a total of thirty-six complaints from unhappy ex-customers of yours, Mrs Prendergast. Very unhappy. And if they've seen what I have of this so-called business, I can quite understand why.
TREVOR	Is that her name – Prendergast?
JOANNE	Didn't you know?
TREVOR	I knew it wasn't Buckingham.
JOANNE	Fiona Florence Nightingale Prendergast.
TREVOR	Never!
FIONA	I *am* still here, you know.
CHADWICK	But not for very much longer, if I have anything to do with it. Oh well, I'll wish you good night. Mustn't keep the chauffeur waiting, must we?

MUSIC – *On the Street Where You Live* **(from 'My Fair Lady')**

SCENE 18. *Outside Trevor's House. Midnight.*

JOANNE	Well, here we are.
TREVOR	Yes, here we are.
JOANNE	I had a great time. Best night out for ages.
TREVOR	Did you really? It wasn't bad was it?
JOANNE	Especially that Chadwick. The look on his face when he saw us two. He was doing goldfish impressions for ages. It's Fiona I feel sorry for though. He seems to have given her a right old runaround.
TREVOR	I expect he was only doing his job. If all those people had been complaining.
JOANNE	It was all pretty underhand. Pretending to be wooing her when all the time he was collecting evidence. That was really mean. Well, I suppose we should say goodnight.
TREVOR	Thanks for seeing me home.

JOANNE	My pleasure.
TREVOR	Mother'll be in bed. She always goes up after News At Ten.
JOANNE	Better not disturb her then.
TREVOR	Will I... I mean, can I... you know, go out with you again?
JOANNE	Course you can, Trevor. But look, that's all it will be. Two friends, going out for a laugh. Nothing... romantic. Do you understand?
TREVOR	I think so.
JOANNE	You're a really terrific person, Trevor. You've got a lot more going for you than a lot of men I know.
TREVOR	(*Getting upset*) I knew it would end up like this. I told you it would.
JOANNE	No you didn't. You said I wouldn't want to see you again. And I've just told you I'll be very happy to see you again. Really I will. Look, Trevor, it didn't say on my details but Unreliable's my middle name. You need someone far more settled than I'll ever be. Believe me. So, are you going to cheer up and give me a little goodnight kiss? (*Pause*) Trevor!
TREVOR	(*Subdued*) All right.
JOANNE	Goodnight.
TREVOR	(*He kisses her on the cheek*) Goodnight.

MUSIC – *Night And Day* **(Ella Fitzgerald)**

SCENE 19. *Fiona's Outer Office. Beverly is typing.*

FIONA	(*Groggily*) Morning, Beverly.
BEVERLY	Actually, it's afternoon. Ten to three.
FIONA	Oh, God. I feel awful.
BEVERLY	Didn't the brigadier live up to expectations?

FIONA	You could say that. Look, Beverly, you know what we were talking about the other day. Making ends meet. Well, I think we need to... look, you couldn't possibly put the kettle on, could you, there's a dear? And a couple of aspirins to go with it.
BEVERLY	Rightio. There's a couple of messages for you. Oh, and Trevor called in. You know, the new one.
FIONA	Don't tell me. He wants his money back and is suing me for living off immoral earnings.
BEVERLY	No. He was bringing in a photo – for his details. I did offer to see if you were available but he said you probably wouldn't want disturbing.
FIONA	Very thoughtful, I'm sure.
BEVERLY	He seems really nice. I was telling him about my Tupperware parties. I think he might come to one. Apparently, he used to do quite a bit of cooking himself.
FIONA	Yes, Beverly, but...
BEVERLY	And he was saying he's got one or two little suggestions for you. About the agency. Says you ought to make it a selling point, this trial dating thing. To help get people started.
FIONA	Beverly, you see the thing is – there probably won't be an agency for much longer. There seem to have been a few complaints... about the computer, and...
BEVERLY	Yes, that was the other thing. Trevor's got this friend who knows all about computers. He can fix us up with something. Second-hand probably, but perfectly reliable. I can do word-processing and databases. We can even have our own web site – fbi.com!
FIONA	But it's not just the computer I'm afraid. You see, 'Brigadier Chadwick' as he called himself, was...
BEVERLY	And Joanne phoned. It was a bit complicated so I had to write it down. 'Don't worry about the TSO' whatever that is. 'She's told Montgomery that if he doesn't keep

	mum, she'll spill the beans to *Mrs* Bartlett.' She said you'd understand. Fiona? Are you all right? Fiona?
FIONA	Yes, thank you Beverly. Perfectly all right. In fact, I think a little celebration may be in order. What would you say to some almond macaroons?
BEVERLY	Sorry, I've got a hair appointment at three. I've, er, got a date this evening.
FIONA	Oh, that's nice.
BEVERLY	We're going out for meal.
FIONA	Anywhere special?
BEVERLY	Not really. Just a fish and chips. Some place down by the bus station. The Happy Haddock. Do you know it?

MUSIC – *Getting to Know You* **(from 'The King and I')**

Printed in Great Britain
by Amazon